IF YOUR STRATEGY IS SO **TERRIFIC,** HOW COME IT DOESN'T **WORK?**

IF YOUR STRATEGY IS SO TERRIFIC, HOW COME IT DOESN'T WORK?

William S. Birnbaum

amacom
American Management Association

This publication is designed to provide accurate and authoritative information in regard to the subject matter covered. It is sold with the understanding that the publisher is not engaged in rendering legal, accounting, or other professional service. If legal advice or other expert assistance is required, the services of a competent professional person should be sought.

Library of Congress Cataloging-in-Publication Data

Birnbaum, William S.
    If your strategy is so terrific, how come it doesn't work? /
William S. Birnbaum.
    p. cm.
    Includes bibliographical references and index.
    ISBN 0-8144-5965-X (hard cover)
    1. Strategic planning. I. Title.
    HD30.28.B58 1990   90-55199
658.4'012--dc20   CIP

Printing number

10 9 8 7 6 5 4 3 2 1

For my folks,
Sol and Blanche Birnbaum.
They've been wonderful parents every step
of the way. And I love them for it.

Contents

Preface

What makes the difference? Why are some business leaders successful at building strong, thriving enterprises, while others continually flounder? Why do some consistently manage a healthy mixture of profit and growth, while others engineer the next layoff? Why do some firms radiate enthusiasm, commitment, and fun, while others leave hardly a memory?

For more than two and a half decades, I've searched for answers to these questions. I've searched as businessman, as entrepreneur, as management consultant.

All along the way, I've found answers. But the last ten years have been the most enlightening. I've spent those years working in strategy sessions with groups of executives from client companies. And each of those strategy sessions was far from just another meeting. Instead, each was an intensive analysis of issues at the very heart of the organization. We wrestled with tough, open-ended questions, like "What business are we in?" and "Who is our customer?" and "Why does our customer buy our product or service?" and "In order to be successful, what *must* we be very good at?"

The client companies I've worked with include organizations of every size, from Fortune 500s to entrepreneurial startups. They represent a variety of industries, including low-, medium-, and high-tech manufacturing, and services, including finance, health care, law, communications, real estate development, and consulting. At the time of its strategy session, each team of managers had its own specific level of success. Some of the companies were healthy, thriving, profitable businesses; some management teams were thrashing about, attempting to reverse their company's decline.

But whether the company was large or small, fat or skinny, plain or fancy, each of the strategy sessions brought me closer to conclusions as to why some managers build profitable, growing, fun-to-work-at enterprises, and why others fail.

There are two fundamental differences. First, successful companies *focus on a limited number of strategies*, and they make sure those strategies deal with issues critical to the success of the enterprise. Second, successful organizations work at *building employee commitment* to the success of the strategies. Thus, strategic focus combined with employee commitment makes the difference between organizations which win and those which don't.

I've divided this book into two parts. In Part I, "Thinking Strategically," we'll look first at the organization's external environment—customers and competition and their interactions in the marketplace. We'll talk about understanding your customers and watching for both opportunities and threats.

Also in Part I, we'll look at the internal environment at your company—your employees, your organization's culture. And we'll examine internal strengths and weaknesses. In both instances, we'll be looking for areas crucial to success, areas where you'll need to focus your strategies.

In Part I, you'll find a number of observations, truisms I've uncovered in my years in the world of business. Those observations will encourage you to examine what's unique about your business and what you'll need to win. Here, you'll find some food for thought and ideas for helping you think deeply about your enterprise.

Then, in Part II, we'll look at the strategic planning process—how to develop the plan and, just as important, how to implement the strategies it contains. Here, we'll emphasize building commitment among those who will implement the strategy once developed—among those who will *make it work.*

I've time-tested each of the ideas in this book. All have survived the scrutiny of rigorous discussion in seminars and workshops, in board meetings, and in strategy sessions.

I hope you will gain from this book and that the truths about competitive strategies I've discovered over the last twenty-five years will help you improve your business, steepen your growth curve, brighten your profit picture—or simply increase your fun factor.

Finally, I'd like to thank my clients. I'm grateful to all of them for all the thoughts on all the issues during all the hours in all the strategy sessions. Because of my clients, I've arrived at the vast majority of the conclusions and ideas you're about to read.

Part I
Thinking Strategically

1

If Your Strategy Is So Terrific, How Come It Doesn't Work?

Most management teams are initially pretty confident about the strategies they develop. Confident their strategies are "just right" and that those strategies will work.

But all too often, something goes wrong. Somehow or other the strategies don't work as intended—if they work at all and if they're implemented at all (too often they're not).

What goes wrong? Management has certainly developed a sufficient *number* of strategies—four for marketing, three for human resources, six for product development, seven for production, two for finance—seems as if they have enough to guarantee success in implementing most, if not all, of them.

The managers who've developed those strategies can well remember their enthusiasm upon completing the plan. With such a complete assortment of excellent strategies, how could they fail? Certainly they couldn't. So the managers who developed those well-thought-out

strategies just naturally assumed that they would work.
But they didn't. Why?

A couple of reasons: First, the strategies lack a consistent focus. There are simply too many of them, going off in too many directions, unrelated to each other, lacking a consistent theme. So they compete with each other for scarce resources.

There's a strategy for reducing the level of finished goods inventory and another for decreasing shipping time—two strategies seemingly in conflict. There's one for improving cash flow, one for increasing R&D expenditures and capital equipment purchases, and one for developing and delivering a training program for employees—again, strategies in conflict.

Clearly, such a large number of unrelated strategies will pull an organization in different directions, each competing for limited resources. So how can management articulate such an array of strategies—clearly describe where it's attempting to lead the organization? How can it rally the troops into action? It can't.

Aside from the lack of focus, there's a second reason why well-conceived strategies too often don't get implemented: Management fails to develop commitment among employees, the folks who must play an active role in implementing the strategies.

Thus, too many well-thought-out strategies are bound in a pretty book that sits in a drawer or on a shelf, infrequently, if ever, referred to. Though the strategies are well thought out—in fact, some are terrific—they simply don't work. They don't even get implemented.

To implement their strategies, managers must realize the need to focus on a limited number of related strategies and the need to build employee commitment for implementing them.

Focus

A company's limited number of strategies must be focused on those key areas critical to the success of the particular enterprise. Professional service firms (accounting, law, consulting) had better focus on practice development (a fancy way of saying *marketing*) and on delivering excellent service. Containment of expenses is of secondary importance to such firms. Although necessary, cost containment is not critical. Professional service organizations can afford to be average in this area, but they'd better be excellent at practice development and delivery of service.

Likewise, in a high-technology startup, technological development and capturing market share are crucial. Production efficiencies are less important. They will *become* important, but later, when the product reaches maturity—not during startup.

Commitment

Management needs to recognize the importance of running its planning process in a manner that develops commitment to its strategies among those employees who assist in developing them, as well as in those who will play an active role in implementing them.

But far too often, managers make the mistake of leaving strategy implementation until after they've developed their strategies instead of beginning early, with the selection of the right members of the planning team, with the solicitation of ideas from throughout the organization, with the gathering of information necessary to successful strategy development, and with communication—not as an "event" such as a single memo or a brief meeting but as an ongoing managerial process in support of successful strategy implementation.

If there are any secrets to getting strategies to work, they are these: First, develop a limited number of *related* strategies; get them all pointing in the same direction so that they support each other rather than pull in opposite directions and compete for resources; make sure they point in not just any direction but toward success in crucial areas.

Second, build commitment; get people to care, to want the strategies to work, to think about the strategies as their own. Begin building that commitment as early in the planning process as possible, well before developing your strategies.

2

What Are You Doing That's Different?

One Southern California entrepreneur decided to launch a business attempting to take "a few percentage points" of market share from the industry leader. *Seems simple,* he reasoned. *Since the leader has 65 percent of the market, he'll hardly miss only 3 to 5 percent. And that 3 to 5 percent should result in a nice little business for us.*

Well, market leaders really *do* notice losses of "only 3 to 5 percent." But keep reading. Things get worse.

The entrepreneur copied the leader and developed a "me too" product and a "me too" marketing strategy. *To give the consumer a choice,* he reasoned.

Result: dismal performance. The company was soon drained of capital—and energy. The investors were quickly soured. Threats from lenders followed. And after a few strenuous years, an exhausted entrepreneur closed his business.

What was the problem?

The problem was that the entrepreneur's thinking was fundamentally wrong. He failed to respect adequately the industry leader. He underestimated how terribly difficult it is to take even a little bit of market share with

7

a "me too" strategy. As is usually the case, the leader was firmly entrenched in the marketplace.

Solidly positioned in first place in the minds of customers, leaders enjoy a far greater market awareness than do newcomers in their fields. Like Coke and Xerox and Kleenex, the leader's name is first on your mind when you think of the product or service. Sometimes it's true and sometimes it isn't, but prospective customers generally assume the market leader offers better products and services than its smaller-share competitors. And when customers are forced to choose among competing products or services they don't fully understand, the leader's brand provides the safe decision. Thus the powerful position of IBM in office automation.

The leader's entrenchment is indeed firm. Leaders are tough to beat. The rich get richer.

Faced with such formidable competition, what are smaller or newer entrants to do? Must they simply stay out of the market? Or is there a way in?

Sure there's a way in. But the way in isn't to copy the leader's marketing strategy. The way in is to *do something different.*

Market newcomers have three choices: differentiating product or service, focusing on a specific market segment, or changing the rules of the game. For example, Johnson & Johnson's toy division decided to differentiate its product from the competition by selling infant toys by direct mail and as a series—kind of a toy-of-the-month. Also, the company included educational material for mom and dad to teach them how to stimulate Junior. Think about it. First-time parents don't know how to help Junior. Along comes J&J to help.

Cessna focused on a specific market segment. It opened "Hanger 10" stores in shopping malls to sell pilot supplies and flying lessons to young affluents more likely to show up in the mall than at Cessna's hangar on the far side of the airport.

Spinnaker Software also focused on a specific market segment, educational software for children. Management figured out it's the moms who make the decisions regarding the kids' education. The moms were the target. So instead of advertising in personal computer magazines, Spinnaker advertised in *Better Homes and Gardens* and *Good Housekeeping.*

Rosemont Engineering Company changed the rules of the game with its market launch of Rosemont's ski boot back in the 1960s. The company raise-lettered its name, "ROSEMONT," in big, bold letters across the bottom of its boot. But it *reversed* the letters—so the wearer of the boot imprinted "ROSEMONT" all over the snow. Imagine that, imprinting the company name all over the snow! Why, nobody had ever done that before. Rosemont changed the rules of the game.

Whether differentiating product or service, focusing on a specific market segment, or changing the rules of the game, successful smaller companies are *not* copying. They're innovating, exercising entrepreneurial flair. Yes, they're taking a risk—and winning.

3

Why New Products Fail

Estimates on the percentage of new products that fail run as high as 80 percent—a surprisingly high number.

You'd think a far greater percentage would succeed, wouldn't you? After all, the majority of new products are launched by otherwise successful companies. Companies operating profitable businesses, offering ongoing, successful product lines.

And most often, companies that launch new products commit significant resources. They make use of market research, invest in capital equipment, and employ intelligent, hardworking people.

And yet their new products frequently fail.

They fail for a variety of reasons. Often, they fail because of unfavorable trends in the marketplace—like tough competition or changing customer preferences. Or they fail because of some destabilizing external event, such as economic turbulence, a war in the Middle East, or government regulation (or deregulation) of a particular industry.

But more often, the failure is caused by some far less destabilizing *internal* factor. Often the new product simply doesn't fit the organization attempting to launch it along one of three dimensions—*marketing, opera-tions,* or *technology.* These dimensions are represented by the three corners of Triangle A in Figure 3-1.

Triangle A represents the company's existing product line, and Triangle B, the new product. How different is the second triangle from the first? If each of the corners were located in exactly the same place, the new product would be nothing more than an extension of the firm's current product line.

If the top corner were different, that would represent

Figure 3-1. Relationship between new and old products along three organizational dimensions.

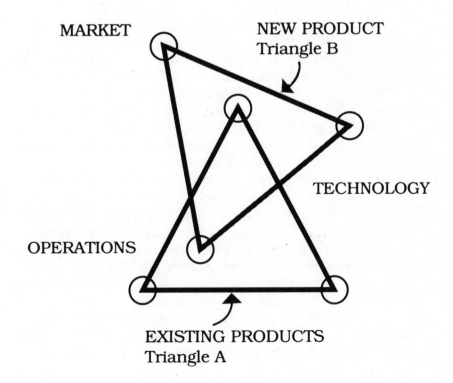

a similar product (same technology and operations) targeted at a new market. A small movement of the upper corner represents targeting a related market; a larger movement, targeting an unrelated market. If the lower right corner were different, that would represent a new technology; the lower left corner, new operations.

Now the big question: For a particular new product launch, how many corners of the triangle are you attempting to move? By how much are you attempting to move each of those corners? In effect, how different is the new product from your existing product in marketing, in technology, and in operations?

Generally, organizations can handle a new product that is different from the old in one dimension only. That is, you expect a pretty good chance of success if only one corner of the triangle must shift to accommodate a new product. You're especially confident if you need to shift that corner by only a small amount. That indicates that the new product is closely related to the old.

Perhaps you can handle a change in two dimensions—particularly if both of the changes are small, and if the new product is related, rather than unrelated, to your current products.

But if you attempt to move two corners of the triangle a significant distance or to move all three corners of the triangle, you're probably asking for trouble. For then, you're trying to operate a very different business alongside your more traditional business.

Because your more traditional business is just that—more traditional—the new product is just different enough that it represents a "no fit" situation. Though significant, the resources (marketing, technology, and operations) you dedicate to the new product are insufficient—or more often, inappropriate—and the new product dies.

And it isn't just product manufacturers that face this problem. Service organizations do also. If you think of "technology" as "expertise" and "operations" as simply "delivery of service," you find the argument works just as well for new services as it does for new products.

And it works for new acquisitions, also. If you're interested in buying a company making a product similar to yours in a similar factory and selling that product to a similar market, you stand a pretty good chance of success. But suppose you're considering acquiring a firm that makes a different type of product, uses a different manufacturing process, and sells that product to a significantly different market. At the very least, that acquisition will present you with a significant challenge.

4

Selling vs. Marketing

A group of executives from a West Coast manufacturing company once spoke with me about their marketing plan. They described their *sales* force, *sales* techniques, and *sales* commissions. I suggested they had a *sales* plan, not a marketing plan.

"What's the difference?" they asked.

Don't be too surprised by their confusion. I wasn't. Lots of managers confuse selling with marketing. But they shouldn't.

Selling and marketing are different. Selling focuses on the needs of the seller to exchange products or services for money. Marketing, on the other hand, focuses on the customer. It's the process by which the seller satisfies the customer's needs.

Sellers must worry about customers' needs because of one important assumption: *Satisfying customer needs will benefit not only the customer, but also the seller.* And this assumption is correct. To see why, compare sales-oriented to marketing-oriented companies.

Managers in sales-oriented companies base decisions on internal information—information relating to the needs of the firm, rather than its customers. Management's insulated from the marketplace by a strong sales force well trained to "push" the product. Thus management lacks specific market information, a general market overview. Existing products, facilities, and skills become

primary; benefits to customers become secondary in determining new product and service development. This
makes the firm slow to respond to market changes. The
company seems never to catch up with competition,
never to please its "finicky" customers.

Marketing-oriented companies base decisions on external information. Such companies monitor changes in
customers' wants and needs, in competitors' activities,
and in related economic factors. Attention to the market
is continuous; information, current.

Market consciousness exists throughout the organization. Top management maintains a keen market
awareness and plays an active role in the firm's relationship with customers. Armed with up-to-date information, the organization stays responsive to changes in
the marketplace.

Sales-oriented companies invest heavily in a strong
sales force. And the sales force works under constant
pressure, hampered by high turnover and management's
continual search for "fresh blood." Sales training programs include "negotiating," "closing the sale," and
"motivation."

Marketing-oriented companies need not invest as
heavily in their sales forces. As they're responsive to
customers' needs, their products and services are better
accepted in the marketplace. Selling is less of a "push,"
less of an intense pursuit. Sure, the sales force should
still be top-notch. But it needn't use high pressure. Instead, the sales force sells with professionalism, focusing
on customer service, not sales tactics; on applications
assistance, not rehearsed sales pitches. This more professional selling style raises the sales force's morale, reduces
turnover, and results in a smaller investment for the
company adopting a marketing orientation.

Selling-oriented companies suffer inefficiencies, like
those caused by inaccurate sales projections. Lacking
information from the marketplace, these companies base
projections on extrapolations from recent history, a
method guaranteed to miss market changes.

Advertising is also inefficient. As a selling-oriented

company lacks full appreciation of customers' needs, advertising fails to deliver a message of actual customer benefit.

New-product and service development also misses the mark. Generated by internal information, new products and services fail to respond to the demands of the marketplace. They simply do not sell, despite the hard (though inefficient) work of the sales force.

Marketing-oriented companies enjoy corresponding efficiencies. Sales projections are more accurate; based on up-to-date information from the marketplace, they are both well-grounded and timely. Their advertising, also more efficient, addresses the wants and needs of a well-targeted market.

Marketing-oriented companies enjoy greater success introducing new products and services developed in response to customers' needs. These companies' catalogs contain active, viable offerings, a sure formula for increasing the motivation and efficiency of the sales force.

The advantages of a marketing philosophy are significant. But managers have to believe, *really believe,* that satisfaction of customers' needs benefits not only their customers, but their own company as well. And it isn't enough just to talk about it. Management has to *do* it.

5

There Are No Customers, There Are Only Relationships

A while back, I worked with the research and development department of a major electronics company in California's Silicon Valley. The organization had been having a terrible time developing products that anyone wanted to buy. One after another, the firm's new products were missing the mark in the marketplace.

From the discussions at the strategy sessions, I came to realize that the R&D engineers were out of touch with the users of their products. So I asked, "During the last year, how many visits to customers has each of you made?" The number of customer visits which each engineer reported ranged from zero to one. Zero to one! No wonder the organization continued to miss the mark in the marketplace.

Clearly, the folks who were responsible for developing new products were out of touch with those who were to use those products. Oh sure, the company did have a sales and marketing department. And those in the sales and marketing department did visit customers. But the sales force didn't develop new products. The engineers did. And the wants and the needs of customers somehow or other weren't accurately communicated between the sales force and the engineers. Without ever intending to do so, the sales force acted as a buffer. It kept the engineers away from customers and, in the end, kept the new products off-target.

It's a pretty typical problem, particularly with highly technical products. I've seen it in my own career.

I grew up in the world of electronics instrumentation, of engineers and high tech, and of product development. As my career advanced from the laboratory to the conference room, I noticed an interesting thing. Whenever prospective customers considered their first purchase of a particular technical product, both the person buying and the person selling had to be educated in the technology of that product. The complexity of the product dictates that communication take place on a technical level—"engineer to engineer," as I call it.

The buyer needs to understand the product's specifications and features and how to apply the product to meet a specific requirement. A customer needs to understand how to use the product, how to maintain, modify, and repair it. This information, in the detail required, can come only from a technical person on the selling side, a person who is truly a peer of the buyer.

This engineer-to-engineer requirement isn't unique to the electronics industry. It's true in other technical fields as well. Medical products, for example, are best sold by peers: by medical doctors or by medical scientists able to look the doctor (customer) straight in the eye and explain, in technical terms, why this particular product is beneficial for that particular application. (The idea applies in nontechnical areas, as well. It takes a management consultant to sell the services of a management consultant.) Because companies frequently ignore this obvious fact, they're often forced to salvage a sale by sending in someone with technical know-how to bail out a nontechnical salesperson.

For example, a technical products company hires a

new salesperson in a particular territory. The new salesperson has good selling skills, but only limited technical knowledge.

The company's advertising generates an attractive sales lead in the new salesperson's territory. The new salesperson goes out to call on the prospect.

The prospective customer expresses interest in the product but needs specific technical information beyond what the salesperson can supply. (It seems there is "something different" about this particular application.)

The salesperson sends four drawings and makes six phone calls back to the factory, attempting to obtain information to satisfy the prospective customer's request for information.

Time goes by. The prospective customer begins to forget about the selling company and the product, and also forgets the name of the salesperson. Suspecting a loss of favor with the prospective customer, the salesperson grows more and more frustrated.

To stress the importance of the prospective account, the salesperson places a seventh call to the factory "a level or two above proper channels." During that final call, the salesperson may even be guilty of an exaggeration or two.

Finally, the salesperson gets some support from the factory. A technical specialist from the factory comes out to visit the prospective customer. During their meeting, the technical specialist and the prospect speak in the jargon of the industry and draw a diagram or two. The salesperson looks on attempting, unsuccessfully, to understand the conversation.

The technical specialist flies home and three days later sends the prospective customer a revised drawing and updated specifications. A week later, the technical specialist calls the prospective customer to converse again in technical jargon.

Then—zippo! Like magic, the salesperson drives by the prospective customer's office to pick up the purchase order.

And that's the way it works. It takes a selling technical person meeting eyeball to eyeball with a buying technical person to consummate the buyer's first-time purchase of a technical product. And anyone else—a non-technical salesperson on the seller's side or a purchasing agent on the buyer's side—will simply get pushed out of the way every time.

That doesn't mean you can't sell technical products using a non-technical sales force. You can. But you should recognize that on the initial sale (and during much of the technical support which inevitably follows), non-technical salespeople are really *finders.* They'll snoop out the prospect, get a rough idea of the potential order size, and tell your technical specialists which airport to land at.

If you expect much more, you'll waste a whole lot of money.

6

Everyone's in a Service Business

I recall the summer I bought my slide rule. I was about to enter my sophomore year in engineering school. I was sure proud of that slide rule. Though I knew just enough to use its most basic scales, I was certainly anxious to apply it in the coming school year.

Then the accident occurred. A couple of weeks before classes began, I dropped the slide rule and shattered the cursor—that little glass window with the fine line scribed on it (you do remember slide rules, don't you?).

I was frantic! With the school year about to begin in a couple of weeks, I was without the ability to calculate. I was in big trouble, doomed to failure—perhaps to death!

In panic, I penned a letter. And I mean *penned* a letter, for as a nineteen-year-old kid I didn't have access to a typewriter. I penned a letter on a plain piece of paper to "Dear Sir or Madam at the Post Slide Rule Company."

My letter said, "I'm nineteen years old, and I'm about to die. . . ." and I was sorry I broke the glass cursor and I needed a replacement. And if Dear Sir or Madam would tell me how I might purchase a new cursor, I would be sure to hurry up and do so.

All this while, I didn't know that the school bookstore sold the darn thing for thirty-five cents, that I wasn't going to die, and that I might make it in life after all.

Seven days after mailing my letter, I received an envelope from the Post Slide Rule Company. The envelope contained a replacement cursor.

So here was this cursor, along with this letter from a fellow who happened to be the marketing manager of the Post Slide Rule Company. He, by the way, did have access to a typewriter. He said that he was sorry that the accident occurred. "Here's a replacement—no charge—thank you very much for using our products and best of luck in the coming school year."

Now the Post Slide Rule Company was in the business of selling *products.* But its marketing manager taught me something about how we have to *provide service* if we're going to keep our customers faithful to us.

About five years later, I was in a position to specify drafting supplies for the engineering firm I then worked for. Can you guess what percentage of the drafting supplies I specified were purchased from the Post Slide Rule Company? A whole bunch. In fact, I needed a very significant reason not to give the full order to that company every time.

It was many years before another manufacturer supplied me with that kind of service. But it did happen again. I had ordered four monogrammed ski bags, one for each member of the family, when my youngest son decided he didn't like the color of his bag. I called the manufacturer, Lands' End. A friendly voice told me, "Send it back and we'll replace it. No charge." When I returned the ski bag, I enclosed this letter:

Lands' End
2 Lands' End Lane
Dodgeville, Wisconsin 53595

Ref: Customer #1082-6135-5 71
      Order   #7069700-0

Dear Folks at Lands' End:

Oh the unpredictability of a seven-year-old!

All four ski bags arrived just as I ordered them. It's just that Dougie decided he doesn't like red. So now I need the monogrammed initials "DAB" on a *black* ski bag. Here's the red one.

When I called you yesterday, Judy said there'd be no charge (other than shipping) for this service. But in all fairness, I think you should charge me something. If you should decide to, please use Visa Card #xxx-xxxx-xxxx-xxx.

Thank you very much.

Very truly yours,

Bill Birnbaum
WSB:lmb

encl: Red ski bag
       Copy of Order #7069-700-0

Five days later, a new black ski bag arrived in the mail. Complete with monogramming. No charge. I've since done a lot more business with the folks from Lands' End.

7

Serving a Derived Demand

Companies which supply capital equipment (equipment used by businesses to manufacture a product or supply a service) observe extreme cyclicality in the demand for their products. In fact, their businesses can virtually dry up during economic downturn.

There's a fundamental reason for these wide swings in demand for capital equipment. Consider a manufacturer of men's shirts who, for quite some time, has enjoyed a continuing demand for one thousand shirts a day.

Suppose the manufacturer has ten shirtmaking machines, each capable of making one hundred shirts a day, or just enough capacity to meet ongoing demand.

If the lifetime of each machine is ten years, the shirt manufacturer will, on average, need to replace one worn-out machine each year. So, to this shirt-manufacturing customer, the supplier of shirtmaking machines sells one replacement machine each year.

Now consider what happens if the demand for shirts drops to nine hundred a day—a 10 percent drop. The demand for nine hundred shirts requires the use of only nine shirtmaking machines. Since the shirt manufacturer now has one extra machine, the company will purchase *no* replacement for the worn-out machine during the next year. This represents a 100 percent drop in machine sales to this manufacturing customer.

If shirt demand levels out at nine hundred a day, the shirt manufacturer will meet production needs on nine machines and will need to replace 0.9 machines each year (actually, the company will buy a whole machine every thirteen months or so). Note that machine sales have leveled off at 10 percent below their original level—matching the percentage drop in the demand for shirts.

About the time things look as if they're leveling off, the demand for shirts goes back up to one thousand a day. Well, the shirt manufacturer now needs one new machine, bringing him from nine to ten, because of the increased demand for shirts, and another to replace the one worn out during that year. Thus, the company will need to buy two machines during the year of recovery. At exactly the same level of shirt production (one thousand a day), the manufacturer will buy *twice* the number of machines purchased in prior years, and twice the number the company will need to buy in future years if demand again stabilizes at one thousand shirts a day.

Economists call the demand for capital equipment a derived demand. A derived demand is one that exists only because the demand for an end product exists. No one would need shirtmaking machines if no one needed shirts.

That suggests something important. Suppliers of capital equipment can best get a handle on their business by monitoring the demand for their customers' end products, by knowing about as much about their customers' businesses as their customers do, and by helping their customers become more successful in producing their end products.

Many in the service industries enjoy a derived demand, too, providing a service only because an end user needs their clients' products and services. Whether they

provide airline seats, conference center rooms, or consulting hours, all are highly dependent upon a derived
demand. Those in service industries had better be watchful of their clients' needs to serve that end user. And
they had best prepare for occasional volatility in their
own service businesses.

8

The 80-20 Rule Works Only 80 Percent of the Time

If you're growing a row of flowers, you'd like them all to look pretty, nice and even with rich color. So you'll water them all, fertilize them evenly, in an effort to make sure they all make it.

But if you breed race horses, your strategy is entirely different. You buy a few, breed a few, train them all, until you discover you have an exceptional horse, a winner. Then you pour all of your resources into your winner.

In running your business, you've got a choice. You can manage as if you're raising flowers—or as if you're raising race horses.

You can invest resources in an attempt to make the non-bloomers bloom, get them all even, and make sure they all make it. You can invest resources in fixing your weak products, your weak markets, and your weak employees.

Or you can invest your resources in the winners, in making your fastest horses run still faster. In other words, you can pour resources into your winning products, your winning markets, your winning employees.

There's a strong tendency to run businesses as if the managers were growing flowers—to direct resources toward obtaining a similar return on every product and investing more in low-performing products, markets, and people.

This management by exception is *wrong*. For business is a lot more like horses than flowers. Your strongest products, markets, and people are most responsive to the investment of additional resources. That's where your maximum payback occurs.

So when your marketing people tell you they've come up with one more idea to revitalize that poor-selling product, tell them to forget it and to spend their time thinking up a way to sell still more of your better-selling products.

Here's where the 80-20 rule on the relationship between input and output comes in.

The 80-20 rule was developed by Vilfredo Pareto (Italian, 1848–1923), who gave it the formal name of the Law of Maximum Ophelimity. Today, that hard-to-pronounce law is more commonly known as Pareto's Law, or simply, the 80-20 rule. Briefly stated, the law claims that "80 percent of the output comes from 20 percent of the input."

While Pareto's fields were economics and sociology, his law applies to the business world pretty well. For example, 80 percent of profit generally comes from 20 percent of the products or services offered. Figure it out for your own business. It fits, doesn't it?

And 80 percent of quality problems come from 20 percent of the components, sub-systems, or suppliers. They're the recurring problems that managers "solve" over and over.

The law works for people, too. Eighty percent of employee problems come from 20 percent of the employees. Close your eyes and you'll see those employees standing before you. About 20 percent, right?

Money, too. Eighty percent of total dollar expense goes to 20 percent of the expense categories. You can check this one quickly. Just glance at your last income statement.

Did I generalize in each of these examples? Sure I did. But more often than not, the generalization is true. The 80-20 rule works pretty darn well as a rule of thumb in many areas of the business world.

The strategy for managing such 80-20 situations is simple. Focus on managing the 20 percent of input that accounts for 80 percent of output. Push the 20 percent of products and services that yields 80 percent of profit. Work on the 20 percent of components, sub-systems, and suppliers that causes 80 percent of quality problems. Redirect or replace the 20 percent of employees that causes 80 percent of employee problems. Be watchful of the 20 percent of expense categories that accounts for 80 percent of total dollar expense.

But be careful. You can't always manage by the 80-20 rule. Because it doesn't always apply.

It doesn't apply when events are linked, rather than independent, that is, when each event is dependent upon the one which preceded it. In those cases, not just 80 percent, but 100 percent of those linked events must be managed successfully.

It's like traveling from Los Angeles to Boston by plane. First you drive your car to the Los Angeles airport. After parking in the long-term lot, you hop on the courtesy bus, which hauls you off to terminal four. You board your plane, sit back to watch a movie, and a few hours later you land at Boston's Logan International Airport. There you pick up your rental car for a thirty-minute drive to your suburban hotel.

Think about the trip you've just completed. You spent about 80 percent of your travel time in the airplane. Certainly you covered well over 80 percent of the mileage by plane and spent about 80 percent of your travel expense on the plane as well. But that didn't mean you needed to manage only that (80 percent) portion of your trip. You had to manage every single leg of the trip right down to the airport parking lot courtesy bus, whose six-minute, mile-and-one-eighth ride we all take for granted. The events were linked. Each had to be successful if the whole project (getting from Los Angeles to Boston) was to be successful.

In the business world, many projects require the successful completion of each of a number of linked events. As an example, consider executing a contract. You've got to select the contracting party, develop the terms and conditions of contract, and make the proposal. You've got to consider the other party's counterproposal. Then you analyze and negotiate. Then you shake hands. Then you explain the whole thing to your attorney, and to the other party's attorney. Next you draw up the contract and explain to the attorney again. Then you draw up the contract again. Then you sign the contract and get the other party to sign the contract. Then you shake hands again. Then you do what you promised to do in the contract.

You can't do just 20 percent of these steps right, because all of the events are linked. Each one depends on those preceding it. You've got to manage all 100 percent.

Consider the hiring of a key employee. You've got to search for the right person. Contact and interview the candidate. Ask questions. Answer questions. Think about it. Ask some more questions. Answer some more questions. Think about it some more. Develop and present an offer. Wait. Consider the counteroffer. Negotiate. Shake hands. And write a letter of confirmation. Again, you can't manage 20 percent of the steps. You've got to work on all 100 percent.

Think about developing a new product or service. You first identify a market need. Then you test it for a match with your internal capabilities. You must commit the resources to develop the product or service, begin development, continue development, and keep continuing development. Then you test the new product or service in the marketplace, redesign and retest it, design the market introduction program, complete all drawings and manuals, release to production, release to distribution, and finally, introduce to the market. Again, you've got to manage the whole 100 percent. The 80-20 rule doesn't work here either.

The 80-20 rule is a useful tool to carry around in your managerial tool kit. It works in a whole bunch of places. Use it where you can. But don't overdo it! Because, like any other tool, it doesn't always apply.

Remember—a person whose only tool is a hammer will treat all the world as if it were a nail.

9
Work a Process

About twenty-five years ago, Richard Goedl was just beginning his career as a salesman with State Farm Insurance. One day, he turned up with a revelation. Seems he attended one of those "how to sell" programs that insurance companies are forever holding for their salespeople. There he learned, "Work a process, not a project."

The meaning of that revelation was that to be a successful insurance salesman, he'd have to look upon his business as an ongoing process of prospecting for clients and closing sales—a continuum rather than a series of singular deals. The lesson suggests that one shouldn't get bogged down in the specific details of a single deal. Rather, keep hunting down a continuous stream of new deals, over and over—work a process.

The lesson seemed to make sense to Rich. And it certainly worked fine for him. By "working a process, not a project," Rich built a thriving insurance practice.

Work a process, not a project. We might also say that "ten pennies make a dime." Or that the ball game is won by a series of bunt singles.

The lesson made sense to me too. I still remember it after all these years. In fact, I think of Rich's lesson often. But that lesson isn't a universal truth. In fact, the success of the application of that lesson depends largely on the nature of the activity it's being applied to.

As in Rich's case, insurance sales lends itself to working a process. The successful insurance agent knows that "it's a numbers game." If he makes enough sales calls, statistically, he'll make enough sales. He works a process.

Retail stores work a process as well. They cater to a large number of shoppers, none of whom individually contributes a significant portion of the store's total income. In fact, retailers, particularly those in major cities and suburbs, typically don't even know their customers' names. They work a process.

Mail-order companies also work a process. They send out hundreds of thousands of catalogs, looking for that statistically small percentage of sales they need to make the mailing worthwhile. Again, each individual customer represents a very small percentage of the companies' total revenue. The companies work a process.

Other businesses work a project, rather than a process. One example is insurance companies which insure large, unique assets, such as the Empire State Building or American Airlines' fleet of planes. In these cases, the asset is so large and so unique that a special project must be managed to create a unique insurance policy.

Same thing with mainframe computers. Each might cost $1 million or $2 million. Only a few hundred might be sold in any particular year. Each sale is unique. Each installation is specific to a particular customer's requirement. The sale and configuration of the mainframe computer can be thought of as a specific project.

Here's another example. One particular company manufactures landing gear for military and commercial airplanes. You've got more fingers than that company has customers. But each of those very few customers represents a very significant percentage of the company's total revenue. Each specific contract calls for a unique combination of specifications, pricing, delivery, and sales strategy. Each is clearly a project.

Process vs. Project

Many businesses require the management of both process and project. Typically, management of the process will lead to the management of specific projects. We find this combination applicable in selling high value added goods and services such as Rolls-Royce automobiles. If we were operating a Rolls-Royce dealership, we'd probably begin our sales efforts by managing a process. Perhaps we'd do a mailer (probably a first-class letter) to the affluent folk in our geographic area. But just as soon as Mr. Albert Affluent responded to our mail campaign, we'd "work" old Albert—a project.

The same thing is true in selling investment opportunities (high-priced ones), legal services, and consulting services.

In each case, the process represents the finding of the prospective customer (or client). And the project represents the conversion of the project into a customer (or client) and the delivery of product (such as a Rolls-Royce with a custom paint job) or service.

Managing a process requires a different set of skills from managing a project. And typically, the same people won't do an equally good job at both. Those who do well in managing the process have what I call a "horizontal focus." They enjoy doing the same thing over and over again, fine-tuning it to make it better and better, whether they're selling life insurance policies, or running a mail-order business or a retail store.

Those who do well at managing a project have what I call a "vertical focus." They get their kicks from deep involvement in one or a few projects—like selling three insurance policies a year, one for the Empire State Building, one for American Airlines' fleet of jets, and one for the San Diego Zoo.

Each of us, as individuals, tends toward one orientation or the other—horizontal or vertical, process or project. We become uncomfortable in the other mode.

The horizontal folk (with a process orientation) become impatient with the details of major projects. And the vertical folk (with a project orientation) become bored with the sameness of an ongoing process.

And that's fine. We simply must recognize which of the two orientations each specific function of our business calls for, also recognize the fundamental orientation of each of our key employees, and make sure the two match.

Standards vs. Specials

Let's examine another issue that relates to process versus project. That issue is standards versus specials.

Some say that if you are manufacturing standard products or delivering standard services, you should never produce specials in the same factory, facility, or office. Their reasoning is that the specials make major demands on resources, so much so that the specials will require virtually *all* the resources; thus they'll be accomplished at the expense of the standards.

For standards are *process*-related. The nature of the standards business is to fine-tune a process of manufacturing or delivering the same products and services today, tomorrow, and next week—and, over time, to improve quality, efficiencies, and cost.

Specials are *project*-related. Their nature is one-at-a-time. Because each is different from the last, developmental resources are required by each special. And that means specials tend to be "resource hogs." An organization producing both standards and specials on the same production line, or in the same office, runs the risk of having specials use up all the developmental and operational resources, leaving nothing for the standards. In fact, the specials will probably pull most of the managerial focus from standards as well. In that sense, specials will "choke" standards.

One manufacturing company, which at one time had an excellent line of products, was unable to increase sales in its core business because of a weakness in marketing. So, in an effort to increase sales, management decided to reach out for more special products, products similar to those in its catalog, but different by one or more specifications.

By the time specials reached 15 percent of sales revenue, the company was choking on its specials. Engineering was spending all of its time in the "onesy-twosy" business, designing a product of which the company would sell one or two or perhaps three units just once. Manufacturing was rediscovering how to build a new product every time a new special order hit the production floor, forever trying to climb the learning curve, never benefiting from economies of scale.

And because management hadn't figured out why it was choking, its sales department was completely unfocused. Because no one back at the factory had told them it was any harder to develop and build a special than a standard, the company's salespeople freely worked with their customers to specify specials.

And marketing was unfocused as well. If an organization is willing to do "anything for a buck," how in the world do you promote a concept so vague? And to whom?

Worst of all, the organization was spending so much of its resources on specials that its management lost sight of its core business, the handful of older, well-engineered products which still represented the bulk of the organization's sales. Management failed to improve efficiencies in the production of those core products. Thus their costs had crept up, and their gross margins had eroded.

Also, the company was struggling with the development of new standard products. Oh sure, management had identified a number of new products it wished to develop. And the folks in the engineering department had listed those projects on their product development schedule. But to no avail. For specials continued to suck up all of the engineering resources.

Once in a while, a new standard product would come close to launch. And since that product's introduction was way behind schedule, the salespeople would be particularly eager to sell it. So they did. But they didn't sell it as a standard. They sold it as a special. "What's the difference?" you ask. The difference is that as a new standard product, the item required a complete series of tests prior to shipping. As a special, the test requirements were far less stringent. So testing of the new product became far less of a "big deal." Result—the first few shipments of the new product went out the door at lower quality. "And," reasoned management, "since we shipped those first units to meet those lower test standards, why can't we ship the next group (and the next, and the next) to those same lower standards as well?" And they did. For they were so terribly busy working on three more specials at the same time that the suggested short-cut was most welcome. The quality of their product suffered as a result.

To improve quality, the organization had to commit to cutting specials to a much lower level of production. This required the development of criteria for a system for selection of specials. Next, the company had to refocus the engineering resources freed up by eliminating the bulk of the specials on improving its existing line of core products, taking five major products which accounted for the bulk of sales and significantly reducing their manufacturing costs. Next, management had to "protect" the engineering department and insist that a specials overload would not get into the way of reducing manufacturing costs of the core products. That meant strict monitoring of the selection of new specials.

Finally, after significant improvement in the manufacturing costs of the core products was accomplished, management developed a *short* list of new products for development and again protected its engineering resources from a specials overload.

While the example we've just looked at was for a manufacturing facility, those in the services industry are not immune from having to worry about the standards versus specials issue. There's the case of a law firm with sixteen offices. It got to be that size by acquisition. When it wanted to expand into a new geographic area, it simply merged with or acquired a successful firm in that territory. So far so good.

But let's look a bit deeper. The firm was having a terrible time developing strategies which would apply firmwide. That was because each of its sixteen offices had a different specialization—family law in one, business law in another, international trade in a third. No common denominator, no focus, just an assortment of areas of expertise varying from one office to another. Within each of the offices, a specific expertise was a "standard." But from a firmwide point of view, the various areas of expertise were specials. Senior management found it frustrating to try to describe or promote the mission or the identity of the firm or to develop a firmwide strategy.

I once met with a well-respected management consultant in Southern California who proposed that he and I merge our consulting firms. Naturally, his proposal prompted a number of questions on my part.

One important question was what he intended the focus of our joint practice to be. Specifically, what services would we offer to clients? As the focus of my own practice was (and still is) business strategy, I was prepared to examine his answer in the light of the potential "fit." His answer surprised me. He responded, "Oh, we'll do whatever a particular client might ask us to do." "But shouldn't we have a specialization?" I asked. "No," he replied, "we'd then be leaving too much work 'on the table.'" Since I fundamentally believe in focus, I naturally declined the offer to merge my firm with his.

Recognize the issue here? It's standards versus specials—working a process versus working a project. Focus.

10

Delegating—What? How? And to Whom?

Conventional organization charts offer people outside the company a feel for who does what. But for those working within the firm, organization charts are stifling. They put people into neat little boxes, show who's "higher up" than whom, and suggest that relationships are based on a network of solid and dotted lines. They demonstrate where the official power is in the company.

But *power doesn't count.*

More and more, employees are demanding an increasingly participatory role in their working lives, demanding choices, demanding to be treated, not as underlings, but as partners in the decision-making process. Today's workers are more informed, more intelligent, and more individualistic. They aren't powered into action. They're led.

The picture of leadership isn't drawn with "the boss" at the top of the organization chart. The picture of leadership is one of support. So we need an unconventional organization chart, based on support. (See Figure 10-1.) That chart is an inverted pyramid with the boss at the bottom. Extending upward from the boss are outstretched arms with hands supporting managers a level above.

Figure 10-1. The organization chart.

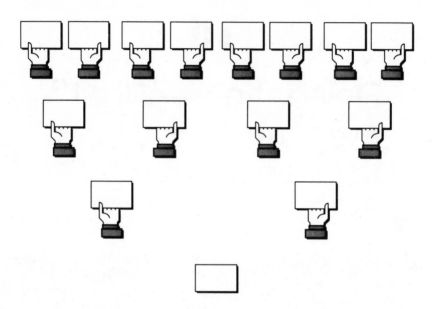

The chart continues in this inverted fashion with each succeeding level of managers supporting the next. Just below the very top are those people "highest up" in the organization—those who actually make the product or deliver the service, those who provide something for someone—*those who actually do the work.* Their hands support the most important folks of all, those at the very top of the chart—*the customers.*

You can add names and titles to the chart if you insist. But I wouldn't. I think the chart itself tells the story.

Through supporting employees, through leading them rather than powering them, through allowing them to participate in decisions which affect their jobs, you'll build their commitment. And there's nothing in the world like commitment for achieving a fun-to-work-at environment and a profitable, growing company at the same time. And also for getting your strategy to work.

What Is Delegation, Anyway?

The most common criticism of managers is that they have an "inability to delegate." And that criticism generally comes from the people who work for the managers being criticized.

What do we mean when we say "delegation"? First, delegation means trust—trusting someone else to do what the organization can't afford to have the manager do.

Next, we have to recognize what can be delegated and what cannot. Proper delegation involves the manager telling the employee what must be accomplished and allowing the employee to decide how to accomplish it. The "what" is the objective that's given to the employee. The "how," which the employee develops, is the method by which that objective will be accomplished.

If properly implemented, delegation offers growth to both parties. For the employee, growth comes from developing the method to accomplish the objective. And the manager grows from learning to trust, to lead, to support.

More often than you'd think, both manager and employee fall into the trap of "upward delegation." That is, the employee gets the manager to offer not only the "what"—the objective—but also the "how"—the method of accomplishment. Not knowing how, or not being willing to discover how, to accomplish an objective, an employee might walk into the boss's office looking for "help." A boss who doesn't handle the situation properly can end up developing the "how," instead of having the employee do so.

That's bad news. Obviously, it keeps the employee from growing. Less obviously, it keeps the manager from expanding his or her ability to accomplish tasks beyond those that can be done by the manager alone.

Instead, the manager must be a leader. That role involves counseling the employee, helping without doing the job of the employee, offering suggestions, support, and trust. The wise manager looks beyond the immediacy of the task at hand and makes sure that everyone in the organization is growing.

Managing by Neglect

I used to frequent a map store in Southern California. There, I'd buy topographic maps for backpack trips to the mountains. A tall, dark-haired woman, probably in her mid-thirties, worked in the store.

And she collected cactus plants. All around the store, on shelves high and low, were potted cacti of many varieties. Those cacti, without exception, were beautiful specimens. Each was remarkably healthy—unusual, too, because cacti generally do far better raised out of doors.

One day, I mentioned to her that I'd been admiring her collection of cacti. I commented that the plants were in excellent condition. "What do you feed them to make them do so well?" I asked. "Neglect," she replied.

Some things, it seems, are better off left to fend for themselves—like cacti. They need soil, and they have to be placed in a pot. But I know from experience (for I too collect cacti) that you can kill them with too much water or even a small amount of fertilizer or sixteen other varieties of well-intended care.

It's the same with some people—those exceptional ones who thrive not on close supervision—for that inhibits them—but rather, on neglect. I don't mean absolute neglect. Even the special few need fundamental support—tools to work with, a comfortable environment, and occasional recognition. But they need—in fact, thrive on—far less attention than most managers are comfortable providing. Such people are best-handled by managers willing to stand back and manage by a rather simple system of informal reporting.

Two factors make for a "cactus"-type employee—one who thrives on neglect rather than close supervision. First, the employee must possess the fundamental skills to do his or her job. That means both knowledge and experience. Second, the employee must also possess initiative—the drive that so often makes the difference between someone who simply does his or her job and the person who shines.

First-Rate People—A Luxury or a Necessity?

Robert Stermer, a former executive with the Rockwell Corporation, has said, "First-rate people hire first-rate people. Second-rate people hire third-rate people."

Bob's right.

Think about it. Haven't you noticed a high correlation between top-performing executives and the top-performing people they hire? Haven't you observed that well-run, successful companies are headed by first-rate executives? Executives who have hired teams of first-rate people?

To first-rate people, the benefit of hiring other first-rate people is obvious. As workers, they don't have to be pushed. Managers simply need supply them with the tools to do their jobs and stand back. Give them enough room, and they're motivated by their own commitment to perform.

As managers, first-rate people have strategic vision. They see the "big picture." They understand the company's objectives and embrace the fundamental strategies necessary to achieve those objectives. Their vision and understanding drive them toward growth.

Yet second-rate people hire third-rate people.

They do so for four fundamental reasons. First, second-rate people lack the judgment necessary to identify third-rate people as such. Since they themselves are second-rate, they're less sensitive to the deficiencies of others.

Also, second-rate people underestimate the importance of hiring first-rate people. Rather, they think in terms of saving a few bucks in salary. Penny-wise.

Third, second-rate people are afraid of being challenged or rivaled by someone they hire, someone better than they are who may eventually get their job. Not only will second-rate people avoid hiring first-rate people, they'll avoid hiring second-rate people as well.

Finally, the best people—the first-rate people—turn down offers to work for second-rate bosses. They look instead for opportunities to work for first-rate bosses, where they will have opportunities to grow.

Here's your choice: You can hire first-rate people and surround yourself with first-rate attitudes, vision, understanding, enthusiasm, and achievement.

Or you can hire third-rate people, put in your eight hours each day, and look forward to retirement.

The Management Triangle—
Hunters, Farmers, and Shepherds

Business managers have predominantly one of three ways of thinking about their enterprises. We can classify those three points of view as those of *hunters, farmers,* and *shepherds.*

Hunters love to go out and "get the business." They're the sellers, the deal makers. Most often, they're content to land the order, drive back to the factory, and "throw the order over the wall." They're perfectly willing to leave building the product, providing the service, and satisfying customer needs to somebody else.

That "somebody else" is the *farmer.* Farmers nurture the "crops"—the company's products and services. Farmers are concerned with quality, with details, with projects and processes. And they're often frustrated by hunters' lack of attention to detail, lack of commitment to the product, and unwillingness to stick around longer than necessary to "throw the order over the fence."

Shepherds are the "people persons." For them, business is as much a social experience as it is an enterprise. Shepherds are easy to recognize. They're the folks who talk about employee training and development. They spend lots of time inviting people to meetings. And shepherds are frustrated by farmers' nose-to-the-grindstone attitude. Shepherds feel that farmers are missing an important dimension—the people dimension—in their work experience.

No manager fits perfectly into any of these three categories. There's some of the hunter, the farmer, and the shepherd in all of us. But each individual is a unique blend of the three. Within a triangle (see Figure 10-2) whose corners represent the three ways of thinking, each individual corresponds to a particular point, closer to one corner than to the other two.

Every company needs a blend of all three attitudes. Each component—getting the order, supplying the product or service, and maintaining the people-relation-

Figure 10-2. The management triangle.

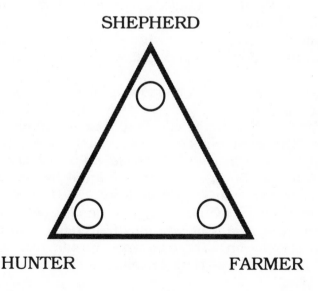

SHEPHERD

HUNTER   FARMER

ships—is necessary for organizational success. All three should contribute to the culture of the enterprise.

Several years ago, in a regional office of a major accounting firm, a particular forty-person department was headed by a partner who was "all hunter." In the parlance of the profession, he focused heavily on "practice development"—on landing new clients.

For the most part, his being a hunter was fine. In the highly competitive public accounting industry, obtaining new clients had become "the name of the game."

But his being a hunter wasn't all good. In particular, it wasn't all good for the managers reporting to him, all of whom needed help in the technical aspects of accounting and in their client relations. They needed help from a partner who had some time for them—who was part farmer and part shepherd. The "all-hunter" partner managing the department was neither.

Fortunately, the partner in charge of the regional office was aware of the problem. He assigned a second partner to "help manage" the department—and that second partner was largely a shepherd. This solution worked—sort of. The newly arrived "shepherd partner" served to remind the "hunter partner" of the needs of the department's managers. The managers' needs were addressed—somewhat. And the effectiveness of the department improved somewhat—but not as much as it would have if the original partner had been a bit more shepherd.

In another case, a consulting firm headquartered in Southern California opened an office in Denver to service the firm's largest ongoing consulting assignment located there. The president of the firm, back in Southern California, looked to the Denver office for business expansion—for obtaining new accounts and for growing into a Rocky Mountain regional office.

But after a whole year, the Denver office failed to obtain even a single new client. It remained a project office, serving only the one large initial account.

The reason was that the manager of the Denver office

was a farmer. Her skill lay in her ability to manage an already-contracted-for assignment. At that, she was superb. But the thought of practice development—of trying to obtain new business—she found frightening. Clearly, she wasn't a hunter.

But a hunter was exactly what the Denver office needed to expand in the Rocky Mountain region.

And the firm did expand in the Rocky Mountain region. But it wasn't easy. The hunters at Southern California headquarters, including the president himself, spent a bunch of time in Colorado drumming up business and getting the expansion off the ground. That expansion would have come far more easily if the Denver office manager had been more of a hunter.

While all three—hunter, farmer, and shepherd—are necessary, be careful. It's tempting to conclude that, ideally, the culture of the organization should be smack dab in the middle of the triangle, that is, to assume its culture must contain equal portions of hunter, farmer, and shepherd attitudes. That isn't necessarily so.

Like everything else in life, it all depends. The correct culture for a particular company depends on its industry. Direct mail and door-to-door sales organizations, for example, focus most of their resources on selling. They're correct in adopting the attitude of the hunter. The name of the game in their business is getting the order. Get the order, throw it "over the wall," and go on to the next order.

Companies in emerging industries tend to be product-driven, particularly during the early stages of their development. They're correct in thinking like the farmer: Develop a "better mousetrap," invent something new, create a new product—a new service, a new marketing channel, or a distribution system.

And many service organizations—in health care, human services, and education—are correct in adopting the emphasis of the shepherd. These organizations deal in a service having a high human-factors content. Theirs is a culture of that revolves around people.

Think about the managerial needs of your own organization and about the tendencies of your present managers. Call a meeting to talk about those needs, and put some dots on the triangle. The shepherds will love you for it.

But make the meeting short. For the sake of the hunters. They'll be anxious to get out and make the next deal.

11

Diminishing Returns

In 1817, the economist David Ricardo (1772–1823) developed the Law of Comparative Advantage. The law explains that more favorable resources will be selected for use first, less favorable resources, later. Thus, return per unit of resource utilized will decline over time.

In developing that law, Ricardo focused on the use of land. He observed, correctly, that farmers attempting to optimize their yields used their most productive land first. Only when the demand for farm commodities outstripped their production capabilities would they begin to use less productive lands, such as rocky areas and steeper hillsides. Naturally, those less productive lands yielded diminishing returns on the farmers' added investment.

Ricardo's law applies to many other natural phenomena. Consider water wells, for example. Increased pumping due to expanding population or a hike in agricultural irrigation lowers the water table. This makes water more expensive to remove from the ground and diminishes the return on investment in drilling and pumping.

Consider the California gold fields. In 1848, James Marshall discovered gold lying on the ground at Sutter's Mill. Those were the good old days. Over time, gold became harder and harder to find. Miners first combed the ground. Then they scratched the earth. Then they picked their way into the earth. Then they blasted. Then they tunneled. Then they spent millions and millions of dollars on modern mining equipment (also made from materials wrenched from the earth). Every step of the way—diminishing returns.

Ricardo's Law in the Business World

Ricardo's principle of diminishing returns applies in the business world as well. Managers encounter diminishing returns whenever they attempt to utilize too much of a single resource disproportionate to other resources.

Think about personnel. People represent the most obvious diminishing return. Sure, you can get more work out of your staff by asking them to work overtime. And you can do that a little bit. Enough to get 10 percent, or 15 percent, perhaps 20 percent more work accomplished. And you can do it for a while. A week or two. A month perhaps. But not much longer. People can't sprint forever. Diminishing returns.

Consider selling. You may begin with an excellent prospect list. Attempt to sell to those prospects—in person, by phone, or through the mail. Keep doing it. You'll note that, after some time, your returns will diminish. The well is going dry because you've already sold to most of the real live prospects on the list. You've picked up the nuggets lying on the ground. Now you've got to scratch away at the earth.

Think about production. Automating production is often an excellent strategy. Automation improves production rates, reducing costs per unit, thus making the company more competitive. Typically, it also increases product quality through improved process control.

But too much automation leads to inflexibility in the organization. A product that must be manufactured "just like this" because "we've got a big investment in tooling." Or a product or service we're "stuck with" because we've got such a large investment in automated equipment that we can't afford to stop. Overautomation can lead to an organization setting strategy based on what piece of equipment happens to be sitting on the factory floor, rather than on what the customer wants to buy.

Consider finance. Adding debt to the company's capital structure may make lots of sense. Financial leverage can improve return on equity—to a point. Too much debt increases the level of debt service (payment on loan) necessary, thus diminishing returns. More significant, the added debt payment increases the firm's vulnerability to economic downturn.

Clearly, you've got to invest resources and take risks. That's what business is all about. But keep Ricardo's principle in mind. And make sure your invested resources are in balance—that you're not investing in one resource disproportionate to the others and that you're not inviting a diminishing return on your investment.

And Don't Get Fat

A few years back, *The Wall Street Journal* reported results of the WSJ/Gallup survey of 822 top U.S. executives. That survey questioned the executives on their feeling about the recession that had recently ended. *Seven out of ten thought the recession was a good thing for the country!*

The surveyed executives said, "It was a well-justified adjustment." "Perhaps it was just the medicine that we needed." "It put a dose of reality into our lives—sharpened us up."

Let's reflect on the specific lessons learned from recessions—on the ways recessions "sharpen us up."

Surely, many of the 822 surveyed executives were from companies that had layoffs during the recession. Whom did they lay off? Good people or deadwood? If they were deadwood, why in the world weren't they booted out *before* the recession?

Surely, a number of the 822 executives narrowed product lines during the recession and discontinued products and services that weren't quite making it, focusing instead on the "real winners." If so, why were they hanging on to the "real losers" before the recession?

I could go on to ask about tolerance for unprofitable activities, belated make-versus-buy decisions, mismanaged marketing programs. But I won't. I've already made my point: During a recession, things get so terrible that business managers finally stop doing the things they never should have been doing in the first place, *even before the recession.*

Managing their business in times of prosperity, executives have their choice. They can hang on to a few weaker products and services, a few marginal activities, a "monument to management" here and there—put on a few extra inches around the middle management.

Or they can act as they were forced to act during the recession. They can run lean—insist on winners only.

Such a policy makes sense for two reasons. First, that's how to grow profitably when times are good. Second, that's how to remain prepared for times that aren't so good.

Prediction: Eighty percent of American business executives will forget the lessons of past recessions and will put on that "extra weight." Until another recession. Then there'll be another article in *The Wall Street Journal* describing the results of a survey, entitled "What 822, or So, Top Executives Have Learned From the Recession."

12

What About The Smaller Company?

For decades, smaller companies have attempted to learn from larger organizations and tried to imitate them in the various functional areas.

In marketing, smaller firms attempted to create the image of larger companies. In manufacturing, they worked toward the efficiencies of economies of scale, toward standardization of product, and toward larger production runs. In administration, smaller companies often modeled their policies on those of more formalized, larger firms.

And the boards of smaller companies often drew their outside directors from the executive ranks of the giants of American industry.

Some of the lessons learned were appropriate to smaller organizations. Economies of scale (at the correct level) do work, a planning process does keep organizations on course, and adding outside directors to the board is healthy as well.

But other lessons learned were not appropriate to smaller organizations. Formalized internal communications systems, for example, destroy a major strength of smaller organizations—their close-linked, informal communications.

Fat personnel manuals, too, are overkill for smaller companies. They offer diminishing returns, causing smaller firms to spend unnecessary resources on policy development and building bureaucracy at the same time.

The drive toward standardization of product and service is also wrong for smaller organizations. A major strength of smaller companies is their flexibility—their ability to satisfy individual customer needs and to supply non-standard products and services. Sure, it's enticing to go for the cost and marketing advantages of supplying standard products and services. But it's a trap for smaller organizations, a sure way to get clobbered by larger, deeper-pocketed competitors.

It's been a mixed bag; smaller companies have learned both good and bad things from larger organizations.

Bigger Is Not Necessarily Better

Now the tables are turning and larger companies are learning from their smaller cousins. Look carefully and you'll see evidence everywhere.

Larger firms are discovering they can't be all things to all people. They're divesting themselves of businesses which don't fit their corporate mission, they're sharpening their focus, discovering the need to segment their marketplace and to copy the "nichemanship" strategy of smaller organizations. Texas Instruments learned its lesson the hard way in the personal computer business and retreated to concentrate on its long-established position in the industrial electronics market. Similarly, General Mills sold off its toy and fashion divisions and returned to its basic products—to Bisquick, Cheerios, and Wheaties.

We're hearing a lot about *intrepreneurship*—about breaking corporate entities into smaller units, each with a product or service, a well-identified market segment, and an *internal entrepreneurial* champion whose mission is to win. Like IBM's facility in Boca Raton, Florida, where a small group of internal "crap shooters" created IBM's PC business far from the bureaucracy of Corporate Big Blue.

Consider the comment from Robert D. Haas, president of Levi Strauss: "This company is guilty of being too rigid and too deliberative in an industry made up of entrepreneurs who hustle. And we're going to have to change." No wonder Levi Strauss established a new entrepreneurial venture—a "fledgling apparel business"— by sending a team of intrepreneurs away from the posh corporate office in San Francisco.

Larger companies are buzzing with the concept of "close to the customer." They're talking about listening hard, being responsive to wants and needs—the very thing that smaller companies have long had to do to survive.

Even in manufacturing, long the stronghold of "bigger-is-better thinking," corporate giants are learning that smaller production units offer significant advantages. These include greater flexibility, improved communications, and an increased sense of employee self-worth. Result—increased productivity.

General Electric Company, having discovered the inefficiencies of running a giant factory, slashed employment at its huge Appliance Park in Louisville, Kentucky, and moved production to smaller facilities. AT&T closed large assembly lines at its Western Electric Company subsidiary (renamed AT&T Technologies) and moved production to smaller, automated facilities.

Prediction: We'll be seeing more of the same. Larger firms will learn more and more lessons from smaller companies as a result of a number of economic factors now at work that will continue—even accelerate—the growth of this important trend.

One major factor encouraging the growth of smaller production units is the existence of maturing markets in maturing industries. This trend increases the need for companies to target segmented markets if they are to survive. An example is smaller steel companies focusing on narrow markets, such as specialty steel alloys. The result is smaller volume, higher margins, and a higher percentage of profit.

Another factor fostering change is overseas competition for high-quality, standardized products. Demand for such products is driving American producers toward specialization and customization; again, segmentation. As an example, in the semiconductor industry, Japanese competitors are supplying (at low cost) the basic building blocks—digital memory chips—while domestic suppliers are developing custom circuits.

Another factor—computerization and the information revolution—is moving industries from capital to people intensity—that is, from an emphasis on manufactured goods to an emphasis on people's skills. While larger companies are capital intense, smaller companies are people intense. In an information age, our economy moves less product, more information. This requires smaller amounts of capital and more people skills—a strength of smaller organizations.

Speaking of people, the fact that larger companies are learning from smaller ones suggests that managers with smaller-company experience may become more valuable to larger organizations. Perhaps we'll see a trend toward election of smaller-company entrepreneurs to boards of larger corporations.

The Family Business

Many smaller companies are family-owned and managed. While some are well-managed, they're the exception. All too often, family-managed businesses are poorly managed businesses. Too many of them support younger family members in positions where they shouldn't be. Typically, the founding parent had the entrepreneurial flair—the personal skills and energy—to build the business. Do the children have the skills to continue in Senior's foot-steps? Perhaps yes. But more often, no.

Yet there sits the oldest son as vice-president of marketing or director of information systems. And if he isn't prepared to excel in that position, his presence there creates a number of problems. First, he may be doing a "not so good job." Particularly if he's inexperienced and has never worked any place else but his dad's business. He's "over his head."

Also, he may be standing in the way of nonfamily-member managers wishing to advance. Those other managers, feeling blocked by Junior, may grow frustrated enough to leave the company. Or worse yet, they may hang around and become underperformers themselves.

The family relationship may have detrimental effects on morale, on the culture of the whole organization, and may establish a "we-they" relationship between family and nonfamily managers.

One more problem: Protecting and justifying the family's position in the business can become a primary objective of the corporation, thus diluting the organization's growth and profitability objectives. Watch out.

Try this—but fair warning, it isn't easy.

First, you should resist the temptation to bring son or daughter into the business straight out of school. Let the children get experience elsewhere. They can join the family business after a few years (if they choose to)—when they really have something to contribute. They'll benefit by waiting, and so will the business.

It's advisable to bring them into the company at an appropriate level based on capability and experience. Let someone other than Dad do the interviewing and make the hiring and placement decisions.

And you need to make sure that son's or daughter's advancement is determined by accomplishment, just as for any other employee. Here, reporting to someone other than Dad helps too.

I told you none of this would be easy.

13

Beware of Wall Street

The traditional view of the business decision-making process is that it is totally rational, that management figures out what to do based on an analysis of available alternatives. And there's good reason for this traditional view.

For one, such rational bases for decisions are taught in the business schools. What MBA student hasn't had his or her share of decision tree analysis, discounted cash flow, and marginal cost? Look at the majority of business books, both in academia and in the local bookstores. They are loaded with discussions on market position, effective advertising, and the formula for calculating internal rate of return.

In addition, corporate pronouncements from the captains of industry, whether at trade association meetings, press conferences, or dinner speeches, all support this traditional, logical, methodical, almost "scientific" method of operating the business.

All of this gets reported in the business and popular press, of course. So we all get sold on the fact that the running of American business is very businesslike indeed.

To some extent it is businesslike. Or at least it starts out to be. It starts out with a manager's, or management team's, conscious decision to develop a new product, for example—a decision based on real, "businesslike" facts. The various departments within the organization may very well get about the business of developing that product. The R&D department moves ahead in its development efforts. The marketing department busily researches a number of market segments and develops new distribution channels. And the production department busily changes the production line to accommodate the new product.

And then a funny thing happens. About ten-thirty one morning, the telephone rings on the president's desk. The call is from a fellow on Wall Street who works for a major stock brokerage firm. He's called a stock analyst. What he does for a living is to figure out which stocks investors should buy and which ones they should sell.

"How does he do that?" you ask. He does it by watching the quarterly returns of a few dozen or so companies in an industry. Or perhaps he'll cover two industries. Or three.

Perhaps you're wondering how he can tell what a company's up to and what its long-range prospects are by watching quarterly returns. Well, I wonder that, too. It turns out he really can't. All he can tell is what a firm's quarter-to-quarter financial performance has been. Since he's only a couple of years out of business school, and this is his first job, and he's never worked in any of the industries he's "specializing" in, he doesn't have a whole lot more to go by.

So from time to time, he calls a company president on the phone and ask questions such as, "How come your profits have been declining for the past two quarters?" He listens carefully as the president explains that "we're investing in the future by developing a significant new product and penetrating an important new market."

And then the young analyst asks when the quarterly earnings might be expected to go back up again. He listens politely as the CEO explains that the company's long-term strategy is a part of a three-year plan. Not until the third year of that plan will the investment begin to pay off, but when it does, the return on that investment will be quite significant.

The young analyst explains that three years is an awfully long time to expect an outside investor to hold a particular stock. Maybe the investors should think about selling the company's stock now and buying it back in about two years when the new product will be ready to pay back on the long-term investment. The analyst goes on to suggest that he might recommend that his investors sell the company's stock . . . unless . . . unless the president can figure out how to implement the new product strategy without impacting quarter-to-quarter earnings. "Sure would be nice if you could do that," he continues, "because you do have an obligation to your shareholders. Got to support the price of our stock. You own quite a bit of stock in the company too, as I recall."

Now the pressure is on. The president marches into the R&D department and asks the director of engineering if it isn't just possible to invent the same product using a third less capital. And he marches into the marketing department to ask if it's possible to penetrate the intended market segment without benefit of an advertising budget. And he visits the manufacturing manager to ask if the production line really needs to be automated. One call, perhaps two, from the young analyst on Wall Street, and the company's long-term strategy, if not dead and buried, is seriously compromised.

Worst of all, one of the firm's major competitors is located in Yokahama, Japan. And that competitor doesn't seem to be focused on the short term at all. In fact, that competitor has been making significant investments in capital equipment to automate its own production line. The capital equipment won't pay for itself in three years but will probably require more like seven or eight. But no one's really sure how long until payback, because the Japanese competitor didn't even make a payback calculation. The company just believes that automation is the correct strategy. So it's made the investment.

And the major Japanese bank that invested in that company isn't particularly concerned with the short term either. That bank views its investment as fairly long-term—ten years, twenty, or more. Perhaps forever.

And yet another competitor, this one in the United States, is also making a long-term investment. That other competitor, a smaller company, is privately owned and operated. And while that smaller competitor hasn't nearly as much capital, its owner-managers have been able to focus on the longer term because they haven't any outside investors to satisfy. They understand that by successfully implementing the right long-term strategies, they can create personal wealth. And they've got more than a few quarters to do that.

So the company whose stock is publicly traded is at a significant disadvantage compared with those competitors, both foreign and domestic, who have the luxury of making longer-term investments—unless the company's president has the guts to hang up on the young analyst from Wall Street.

14

SIO

When Dave Hornbaker was vice-president of Trans-Met Engineering Corporation, he gave everyone in the organization an anxious week.

One weekend, Dave placed a dozen or so small but conspicuous signs around the company—on his office door, on his secretary's desk, on the bulletin board in the assembly area, on the blackboard in the engineering lab.

Each sign carried the same message: SIO. On Monday morning, everyone wanted to know "Why all the signs?" and "What do the letters SIO mean?"

Dave offered the same answer to all inquirers. "I'll tell you on Friday," he announced. That week, Dave's drama became the talk of the office. Just about everyone speculated on the meaning of SIO. Did it mean "Security In Office"? or "Succeed In Opportunities"? or "Similar Is Opposite"?

That Friday, Dave called a meeting of all managers. He began by asking the marketing manager, "Have you ever arrived in a hotel to discover you'd forgotten to pack your pajamas? Or your toothbrush? Or your socks?"

The marketing manager confessed he'd forgotten a thing or two a time or two.

"Why don't you make a checklist of things to pack?" asked Dave. "Then, when preparing for a trip, you could refer to your checklist. That way, you'd eliminate the problem of forgetting things. You'd solve it once."

And so the meaning of SIO became clear: *Solve it once.* The managers spent the next thirty minutes or so offering examples of Dave's SIO philosophy as it applied to the various corners of the company. They decided they should probably stop doing battle with an uncooperative employee and instead fire him and seek a replacement. They might stop "fixing" the worn-out milling machine twice each month and instead rebuild or replace it. And they could stop fighting the quality problems of a now-ancient product, declare the product obsolete, and replace it.

It's amazing how much energy in how many companies goes into "solving" the same old problem—again. It's pretty expensive in terms of opportunity lost, because the company's resources are spent, not really solving, not really accomplishing, and certainly not progressing toward a growth objective.

Worse, perhaps, solving the same old problem (again) tends to focus people's attention on problems. That isn't the way to build a profitable, growing company. You build profitable, growing companies by focusing not on problems, but on opportunities. You need to make room for that positive focus by identifying the problem, making a decision, *solving it once,* and getting on with your opportunities—and with profitable growth.

We identify the problems in need of solution by asking questions. For the most useful tool in the business world isn't the computer. It isn't even the telephone. It's the question mark.

The question mark is particularly useful when you need to identify the real problem hidden behind a whole bunch of symptoms. Like this . . .

Mr. A.: What's the problem?
Mr. B.: Our sales have really fallen off.
    A.: How come?

B.:   Our sales force has become terribly ineffective in selling our products in our traditional market.

A.:   Why?

B.:   It seems our customers are preferring more and more to buy our competitors' products.

A.:   Why is that?

B.:   Because our competitors have been coming out with one new product after another.

A.:   Haven't you been doing the same?

B.:   No, our product line is pretty mature. In fact, a number of our products are actually obsolete.

A.:   How come?

B.:   Consciously or unconsciously, we've been taking a short-term view of our business. Milking our old product line and falling farther and farther behind our competitors' product offerings. I guess we're now paying for our earlier short-term thinking.

Bingo! We just got a handle on the fundamental problem.

I learned the value of the question mark from my two boys, Larry and Doug. It's amazing how much kids can learn by simply asking, "Why, Dad?"

Try using that technique in your own business. It will work. In fact, I'm convinced that the manager's most useful tool is the right question at the right time.

Part II
The Strategic Planning Process

15

Strategic Planning Overview

Everyone who writes on strategic planning offers a slightly different definition of the subject. My own favorite definition is based on the words of a remarkable man who, I'm sure, had never seen the words "strategic" and "planning" put together. Abraham Lincoln said, "If we could first know where we are, then whither we are tending, we could then decide what to do and how to do it."

Consider what Lincoln said, place it in question format, and modernize it just a bit. You'll arrive at the definition: Strategic planning is the managerial process which, examining the organization as a whole, addresses three key questions:

1. Where are we today?
2. Where do we wish to arrive, and when?
3. How do we get from here to there?

In the block diagram of the planning process in Figure 15-1, the three key questions correspond to the process steps *Situation Analysis, Objective Setting,* and *Developing Strategy.*

Figure 15-1.   The planning process.

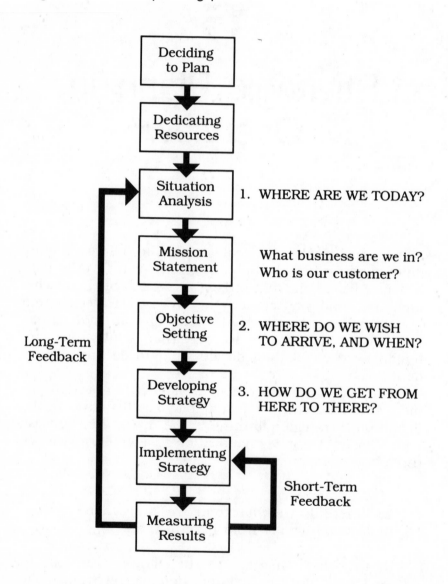

But let's not get ahead of ourselves. Let's review each block in the diagram one at a time. The first block is "Decision to Plan." This makes sense; you can't begin the process until you've recognized the benefits of planning.

Next is a dedication of resources to the process. Nothing in the world is free—and that includes strategic planning. You're going to have to pay the costs of planning, costs that can be measured in terms of people, place, time, and money.

Having decided that strategic planning is beneficial and that its benefits outweigh the costs of planning, you can then begin the process itself with the first *process* step. You begin the situation analysis, tackling the first key question—"Where are we today?"—and examining the organization internally, in terms of its strengths and weaknesses, and externally, in terms of its opportunities and threats.

Following the situation analysis, the planning team next develops its mission statement, a concise declaration of "what business we are in" and "who our customer is." That mission statement sets the stage for the objectives and strategies to follow.

The next process step addressing a key question is objective setting, which involves establishing a handful of quantified objectives that address the question, "Where do we wish to arrive, and when?"

The third question—"How do we get from here to there?"—is considered during the process step called developing strategy. You develop two kinds of strategies: defensive strategies, to solve internal weaknesses that make the organization vulnerable to external threats, and strategies built on strength, to take advantage of external opportunities.

You now have something you can call a strategic plan. You can give it a title, bind it in a pretty book, and communicate it to "the troops." Then the real work begins. Because 85 to 90 percent of your time, work, effort, and probably tears will be involved in the implementation of that plan.

But implementing by itself isn't enough. You've also got to monitor that implementation. Thus, the short-term feedback loop represents a weekly or a monthly updating to discover if you're implementing the plan according to your initial intention.

A longer feedback loop within the planning process goes back from measurement of results to situation analysis where you re-enter the process at the end of the planning cycle, generally one year later. You can think of this as a reset for the strategic planning process.

16

What's So Magic About Five Years?

Many executives refer to their strategic plan as the five-year strategic plan, as if a strategic plan must be for five years—no more, no less.

But there's nothing magic about five years. While five years works well for some organizations, three years or ten years works better for others.

A number of criteria determine the best time span for a strategic plan. First, and perhaps most obvious, is the nature of the business. A utility company planning power substations for future populations requires a plan looking ahead ten, twenty years or more. Companies developing computer software (whose managers sleep wearing running shoes) think three years is forever.

Size of the business also influences time span of the plan. Larger, more mature organizations have resources to commit to longer-range planning issues. Smaller, younger firms, more at the mercy of their environment, must develop shorter-term plans.

Corporate assets and financial structure also influence the planning horizon. A corporation with significant capital equipment or long-term leases is concerned with longer-term issues. Thus, it needs a longer-term plan.

Finally, the external environment influences the time span of the plan. In a time of violently fluctuating interest rates, a company whose business is interest-rate sensitive will find shorter-term plans more useful.

The main question is: How far in advance do you need to plan to run your business intelligently?

Nothing magic about five years.

Well, how about the differences between strategic, long-range, and operational plans? Remember, strategic planning is the process of viewing the organization as a whole in addressing the three key questions: "Where are we today?"; "Where do we wish to arrive, and when?"; and "How do we get from here to there?"

The very nature of those questions is long-range. Thus, the terms "long-range planning" and "strategic planning" are very often used interchangeably. After all, the long-range plan deals, by and large, with strategy and with "mission." In the long-range or strategic plan, the strategies are "broadbrush" rather than detailed. The plan deals with trends, rather than exact numbers "two places beyond the decimal point." The plan is concerned with issues, not the hard, finite numbers to the most minute detail.

Shorter-range or operational plans place *tactics* onto strategies. Those tactics are the action steps—the how-to-do-it, the who-does-it-and-when, and what-are-the-resources-required? Of necessity, the operational plan has a shorter time span than the strategic plan.

Operational plans, far more detailed than strategic plans, are filled with schedules and budgets. They *are* concerned with numbers two places beyond the decimal point. Generally, operational plans have a time span of one year or less. You develop the strategic plan *before* the operational plan. You've got to paint strategies with a broad brush before you detail tactics with a fine point. Planning moves from the more general to the more specific—from strategic to tactical.

17

Approaches to Planning

If you're the president of a company about to develop its strategic plan, you can use one of four approaches. You can choose among the Top-Down, the Bottom-Up, the Top-Down/Bottom-Up, and the Team Approach (see Figure 17-1).

Approach 1—Top-Down

If you choose the top-down approach, you might decide to spend a day or two sitting alone in your office (or living room) writing your company's strategic plan. You'd then have your secretary type your notes as the organization's strategic plan. Next, you'd call in your key people, present the strategic plan to them, and ask their help in implementing it. If you were to take these steps, you would have introduced strategic planning to your organization using the top-down approach.

That top-down approach has both advantages and disadvantages. One obvious advantage is time savings. There's no faster way to develop your strategic plan than to use the top-down approach. After all, as the company

Figure 17-1. Approaches to planning.

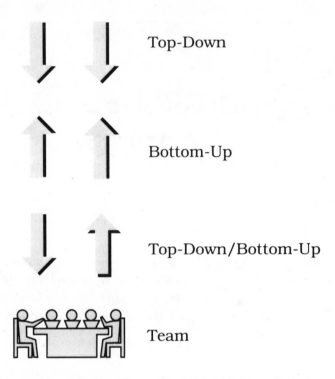

president, you could sketch out all your thoughts in one weekend, have it typed up, and—zingo—a strategic plan!

The top-down approach also ensures your commitment to the plan. After all, what you write down on that lined yellow paper is a collection of your thoughts, your ideas, your objectives. Certainly, *you're* committed.

Low cost is another advantage of top-down planning. One lead pencil, a tablet of lined yellow paper, and a day or so of your time and your secretary's time—that's all that's required. Top-down planning is, without doubt, the least expensive approach to developing your strategic plan.

While the top-down approach has these advantages, it also has some very serious disadvantages. For one, the top-down plan comes from a single mind. One person does it. And while you, as president, probably have the most general management overview of your organization and perhaps the most brilliant mind in your company, or in your industry for that matter, yours is still only one mind. You, like anyone else in your company, simply don't have all the facts. Surely other people within your organization can make significant input to the company's strategic plan.

Probably more important still, the top-down approach lacks managerial commitment. Sure, you, as president and author of the plan, are committed. But no one else is. Other key individuals in your company will look upon the plan as your plan. They've played no role in developing it and thus lack commitment to its successful implementation. This is a very serious problem, because developing the plan becomes quite academic if it can't be implemented.

Approach 2—Bottom-Up

Since the top-down approach has such significant disadvantages, you might choose another method. Perhaps you'd choose the bottom-up approach. Using the bottom-up approach, you'd ask your key managers to hold a series of meetings, or an extended session over three or four consecutive days, to develop the company's strategic plan. And while you'd choose not to attend the meetings, you'd assure your managers that you'll go along with just about anything they come up with, within reason of course.

Bottom-up planning, too, has both advantages and disadvantages. Its main advantage is its collective input. It does come from more than one mind. Although some suggest that through participation, bottom-up planning leads to managerial commitment, it doesn't really. If your managers are developing your organization's strategic plan and that plan is so darn important, how come you're not involved? How come you're not in there with them? If the plan isn't important enough for you to participate in its development, then how important is it really? And how committed can your key managers be?

Also, your managers, in developing the plan, are at risk. Since you, as president, aren't there to speak for or against each decision, everything they decide is tentative, pending your approval. The plan they develop will, therefore, be "safe."

But bosses don't really use bottom-up planning. That is, they don't use it *formally*. They use it *informally*. Presidents of companies don't call in their key managers to say, "I don't have time to develop the strategic plan; why don't you do it?" What they say, *in silence*, is, "I don't have time to develop a strategic plan; therefore we won't have a strategic plan."

Informally, the resultant void becomes filled by others, who "write" the unwritten plan for the company's future. Every thinking manager, in his or her own mind, develops a strategic plan for the organization. The trouble is, each of those unwritten plans is different. For the perceptions of the individual managers are not necessarily in agreement. And as those managers push and pull for their own unwritten plans, the future of the organization becomes rather arbitrary.

Approach 3—Top-Down/Bottom-Up

The top-down/bottom-up approach sounds silly, doesn't it? But it's silly in name only. For this is the method by which planning is typically accomplished in larger organizations. Imagine an organization on three levels: corporate, division, and department. Each of those levels has its specific roles in the planning process (see Figure 17-2). At the corporate level, the organization sets policy and philosophy. At the division level, it develops the mission statement, objectives, and strategies. Finally, at the department level, it creates the tactics, or action steps, by which individuals implement strategies.

These responsibilities of the organization's three levels are clearly related. Divisions must understand corporate policies and philosophies in order to create the mission statement, objectives, and strategies. To develop strategies which can be implemented, the divisions must also be aware of the resources available within their various departments. Finally, the departments must understand divisional strategies before developing tactics

Figure 17-2. Roles of organizational levels in strategic planning.

	Policy Philosophy	Mission Objectives Strategy	Action Steps (Tactics)
CORPORATE	X		
DIVISION		X	
DEPARTMENT			X

to implement those strategies. And this interdependence necessitates ongoing communication within the organization; thus the name "top-down/bottom-up." Because of this need for ongoing communication among all three levels, many of the largest organizations have a staff of corporate planners whose major role in life is to make sure this communication works.

The most obvious danger in this method of planning is its cost. Planning staffs, like all other staffs, have a way of growing rather large. Some years ago, while speaking at the American Management Association's strategic planning course, I mentioned that the largest organizations can have planning staffs of dozens. An executive in the audience smiled when I said that. I asked, "Did I say something funny?" He replied, "Yes." He introduced himself as a vice-president for a major utility company on the East Coast. He asked, "Would you believe that the largest organizations can have hundreds of people on the planning staff?" He said that his organization did.

A second problem can arise from misuse of the top-down/bottom-up model. That problem, fortunately less prevalent today, arises when planning staffs create the plans for the line managers, who are then expected to implement those plans.

In some high-rise office building in New York, a staff planner developed a strategic plan and mailed it to a division manager in Columbus, Ohio. Can you guess what the fellow in Columbus had to say about the plan he received in the mail? Naturally, he questioned the knowledge level of the staff guy who sent him the plan, wondered just how much the fellow in New York knew about the factory in Columbus, and wondered why he, the division manager, didn't get to decide his own strategies.

Naturally, the division manager's commitment to implementing the plan was not too great.

In recent years, managers have learned a lot about developing and implementing strategic plans. No longer are many plans mailed from a staff guy in New York to a line manager in Columbus. Managers now realize that developing the strategic plan is the job of the people who will later implement the plan—the line managers.

While there's an important role for the staff planner, that role isn't to create strategy. Rather, it's to facilitate the process—to communicate, to analyze, to consult. The rightful role of the staff planner is to function as internal consultant for the planning process.

Approach 4—The Team Approach

The fourth and final method of planning is the team approach, in which key people in the organization walk into a room, close the door behind them, and discuss planning strategy for the company. Those key people in the organization include the "boss," whether owner, president, senior partner, CEO, or executive director— whatever the title—and, generally, those people reporting directly to him or her.

The team approach, too, has both advantages and disadvantages. Its advantages include those related to the participation of the company's most important individuals. As it is the highest-level executives who participate, those "in the know" are present to contribute needed information. The plan thus comes from a number of collective minds. More importantly, it comes from the minds of those most knowledgeable—those best able to develop a successful plan.

Just as important, the team approach to planning builds commitment among the key individuals. Because of their active involvement, they feel a part of the plan. They developed it. It's their baby. And that commitment is most important. After all, it's these same top individuals who will make or break the implementation of the plan.

The team approach also has disadvantages. For one, it's costly. Consider the executive time involved. You're taking the top executives from the organization and asking them to spend considerable time in developing their plan. And that's expensive. Think in terms of a typical planning retreat which runs for three or four days. Those few days represent the obvious time. We can fix those days on everyone's calendar and commit to our executives spending that time deliberating at the conference table.

But also consider the "hidden time"—the time spent both before and after the actual planning sessions. Prior to the sessions, executives spend "get-ready" time preparing, studying, researching, analyzing, communicating, and thinking. And after the sessions, those same executives (and others) spend "homework time" cranking numbers, developing tactics, and communicating.

A second, and potentially more serious, disadvantage to the team planning approach stems from the fact that one person, by title, can make or break the planning session. He or she can take over the meeting and turn it into a top-down autocratic exercise. The boss can actually use what appears to be a team planning effort to develop a top-down plan, while the rest of the team simply watches in frustration. The "boss" must appreciate that he or she is participating in a team process. If the other participants are to be committed to the success of the resultant plan, the boss must not take over. The excellent leaders are well aware of this danger and take steps to avoid it becoming a problem.

The president of a medium-size company in Minneapolis told me an interesting story regarding his organization's first experience with strategic planning. On the third day of a three-day session, his planning team was considering two potential marketing strategies. One, which we'll call strategy A, was favored by the president alone. Strategy B was favored by all the other executives on the planning team. Everyone in the room seemed locked into his or her opinion. Clearly, the group was stuck.

After the group deliberated on the issue for forty-five minutes or so, the president realized he had a choice to make. He could have autocratically said, "We've talked about this subject long enough. We're wasting valuable time. We're going to adopt my strategy, strategy A." Or he could have yielded and said, "Sure, I'm the boss, but I respect your overwhelming confidence in strategy B. Let's go with the consensus."

The president made this second choice. He agreed to strategy B. The reason he did so, he said, was because he felt the company would be better off with a second-best strategy that the executive team believed in rather than a first-best strategy that only the president wanted. He was confident that after "selling" the boss on its strategy, his management team would be so totally committed, it would do everything humanly possible to make that strategy work.

Certainly, I'm not suggesting that such a decision is always correct. I'm not even certain that it was correct in this instance. Many factors must be weighed in any particular case. I simply cite the case of a president who recognized the importance of managerial commitment developed through the team planning process.

18

The Benefits of Planning

Why the increasing interest in strategic planning? Obviously, planning offers significant benefits both to the organization and to the individuals involved in the process.

Benefits of Strategic Planning

First, planning forces you to focus on opportunities. After all, you're a busy person. And when you get busy, what happens? You stomp out the brush fires—the ringing telephone, the messages, the meetings, the things that have to be accomplished right now. When you're busy, you become task-oriented.

When you're focusing on the tasks, you're not watching for opportunities. Opportunities have soft knuckles. They knock very quietly. They're not demanding of your time as tasks are. Thus, you tend to ignore them. Planning allows you the time to turn the tasks aside and redirects your attention from tasks to opportunities.

Closely related to this focus on opportunities, planning brings us a heightened market awareness. And that makes sense, for most of our opportunities are in the marketplace. By heightened market awareness, I don't mean market awareness specifically on the part of the person whose title happens to be marketing manager or director of marketing. I mean market awareness on the part of all the individual managers involved in the planning process, all the managers on the planning team. As the key marketing issues are discussed at the planning sessions, all who participate gain a keener appreciation of those issues—a heightened market awareness.

Also, planning increases organizational effectiveness in two ways. First, planning points a direction. People within organizations often have differing, sometimes conflicting, perceptions of where their company is going, which can be detrimental to the firm's effectiveness. Planning forces managers to write down where the organization is going, that is, "where we wish to arrive and when," in the strategic plan and then communicate it to people throughout the organization.

Thus, planning points a direction. And having direction, people within the company can concentrate their resources to "all row in the same direction," thus increasing organizational effectiveness.

The second way planning increases effectiveness is by providing motivation. I'm not referring to the commitment obviously building among members of the planning team. I'm suggesting something well beyond that. I'm talking about providing motivation for people throughout the organization.

I once worked with a mid-sized manufacturing firm in Los Angeles. We had just completed the organization's five-year strategic plan and were about to begin work on its one-year operational plan. The company's executive planning team decided to ask the supervisory-level managers for input regarding objectives for that one-year plan.

Asking for that input was very important for the company at that time because in August of that year, the firm was going to move to a new facility, which meant it would close down the factory for the entire month, pick up all the machinery, load it on trucks, plop it down, wire it up, and go back to work. A good chunk of the month's production would be lost in the process.

This was no small issue for production, no small issue for sales, no small issue for customer service. The company's executives were concerned about the objectives they could realistically set for that first year after the move. Following development of the five-year strategic plan and prior to development of the one-year operational plan, the executive planning team and I made a presentation to the company's supervisory-level managers. We introduced the strategic plan and asked for input regarding the one-year plan and its objectives.

We got back the kinds of answers we went looking for—the opinions of supervisory-level managers regarding the objectives they were comfortable biting off that first year. But we got one more thing, something we didn't go looking for—and that was motivation. The supervisory-level managers said things like, "We're working for a professional organization—we're planning." It seemed that the planning process spread motivation throughout the company.

But it wasn't the planning process per se that encouraged motivation. The supervisory-level managers weren't turned on to their company simply because their executives were planning. Rather they were turned on because their executives asked them, "What do you think?" Their executives demonstrated they cared about the supervisors' opinions.

I like to think my client that year worked on the horizontal line we so often find in organizations—the "we-they line." Most firms have such a line cutting horizontally across their organizational chart. Above the we-they line people refer to the company as "we." Below the line people refer to the company as "they." I like to think that my client was successful at pushing the we-they line a bit further down in the organization.

Planning also increases managerial skills. Earlier I

pointed out that planning increases market awareness. I noted that the increase in market awareness is not solely on the part of the marketing manager. Rather it's an increase in market awareness throughout the planning team, shared by all executives who have an opportunity to participate in the planning process.

There's nothing magic about marketing. We could have made the same argument for production, for finance, for personnel, for each of the functional disciplines. As part of the strategic planning process, the executive planning team deals with all of the organization's major issues. Thus, a broader awareness, a more general management overview, is appreciated by all who participate. And doesn't this say positive things about the potential for growth of individuals within the organization?

One company's executive planning team included the president, a number of vice-presidents, and one other individual just below the vice-presidential level. That last person, then the director of engineering, was invited to participate in the process because he was soon to be promoted to vice-president of engineering. The president saw the planning sessions as a unique opportunity to prepare the director of engineering for promotion by laying out the key issues before him. According to the president, "What better way could we educate Bob to the issues which he'll soon be dealing with? I'm sure he'll come away from this session with a broader outlook for the company and its environment."

Finally, planning allows us an evaluation of alternatives. When we plan, we play a bit of a "what if?" game. For example, we consider "what if" the inflation rate increases, or recession returns, or our major competitor reduces prices? The planning process allows us the opportunity to consider these eventualities and weigh alternative strategies.

One service organization identified its overdependence on a few key accounts as an internal weakness. In response, its planning team developed a set of strategies to aggressively pursue additional business from other accounts. Shortly thereafter, due to economic recession, business from its largest account screeched to a near halt. Fortunately, the service company had, through its newly implemented strategies, captured enough additional business to make up for the loss.

Keep the Process Simple

Some years ago, I received a letter from an executive describing his corporation's strategic planning process. It seemed pretty formal with too much emphasis on process rather than content. At the end of his letter, the executive wrote, "I wonder if we have developed the 'plan' to such a degree that we could be losing some vitality and maybe opportunity."

I replied by asking a series of questions about his company's competitive position, its internal strengths, and the "people dimension" in his plan. I suggested he approach each member of his planning team with these same questions. My intent, of course, was to get his executive team thinking about issues rather than process.

A month or so after receiving the letter, I got a call from a client in a different company. He spoke of a series of highly successful product-line planning meetings that followed the divisional planning session we had held three months earlier. In discussing the strategic planning process and its value as a team-building exercise, he said, " . . . the process is even more valuable than the plan." And I said "yes," because I knew he was right.

But how can the process create a problem in the first case and deliver the major benefit in the second?

Well, there's process and there's process. And they're different.

In the first case (as best I could tell from one letter), the process was a formal, institutionalized taskmaster.

Little wonder it " . . . could be losing some vitality and maybe opportunity."

In the second case, the simpler, less formal process encouraged participation and created commitment among the executive planning team. Here, indeed, " . . . the process is more valuable than the plan."

Organizations which maintain vitality in planning, which are successful in building commitment to their plan, keep the process simple. They encourage contribution and allow flexibility. And they think and act as if they expect as much benefit from the process as from the resultant plan.

19

Hurdles to Planning

If strategic planning is so beneficial, then why are there some companies, and certainly there are, that still don't plan? Obviously, there are reasons why those companies that don't plan don't plan.

The Time Crunch

The first and most significant hurdle to planning is that many executives see themselves as too busy with tasks to take the time to address opportunities. "Go away to a planning retreat for three days?" "All the key executives at the same time?" "Impossible!"

It's a shame they use their workload as an excuse not to plan. Because planning actually makes time for itself. In all companies, people do some of the wrong things, things that lead to ineffectiveness. They hold on to some obsolete products. Or decisions. Or people. Some "monuments to management." This "doing the wrong things" eats up time and resources.

Through the awareness raised by planning, the strategies within the resultant plan, and the commitment developed by the planning process, employees can stop doing some or all of those wrong things. They can recapture executive time, the same kind of executive time the organization earlier invested in the planning process. Thus, planning makes time for itself.

You won't get the time back the first week or the first month. But if you make the right strategic decisions, you'll later recapture all the executive time you've invested in the planning process, and more. Think of planning as a long-term investment.

The Big Unknown—The Future

Another frequently heard excuse for not planning is, "The future is unknown." Since we don't know what the future holds, why should we plan? After all, any strategy we come up with today may well be obsolete two weeks from tomorrow. And there's some truth to that. Because the future is unknown, some of the strategies we develop will soon become obsolete.

But the question to ask is not, "Is the future known or unknown?" The answer to that question is obvious. The right question is, "Given the fact that the future is unknown, are we better off going into that unknown future with a plan or without a plan?"

Planning is sometimes thought of as an intimidating task. And it does *seem* an intimidating task. After all, we're going to ask ourselves a series of challenging, open-ended questions.

But the planning process can be bitten off in bite-sized chunks. We can think of the process in terms of the three key questions: "Where are we today?" "Where do we wish to arrive, and when?" and "How do we get from here to there?" As we follow these process steps, planning becomes not nearly so intimidating after all.

Informational Weakness

Every organization has its own set of internal strengths. Those strengths are determined by a number of factors, including the backgrounds of the individuals who run the company, the company's assets, its market position, expertise, collective education, history, and philosophy. All of the things that affect the organization's character and culture also influence its strengths. High-tech organizations, for example, typically have significant strengths in research and development and often in manufacturing. But internal strengths are just the good news.

Here's the bad news. Those same organizations have an informational weakness somewhere else: perhaps in marketing, perhaps in finance, perhaps in the management of people. This information skew, or talent skew, often stands in the way of planning. An executive team may conclude, "If we know little about marketing, then why in the world should we all go into a room together, close the door behind us, and talk about marketing? We're not going to be any smarter about our marketplace after we're in the room than before we entered." This, too, is an unfortunate excuse. Because there's a simple solution to the informational weakness.

That solution is to bring in an outside resource person, whose skills complement those of the planning team. That person may come either from another part of the same company or from outside the company. That person can then serve as a temporary member of the planning team.

Managers are intuitive, and that can make them uncomfortable about strategic planning. Many business managers like to get up in the morning, strap on two guns, go into the office, and spend the day shooting at anything that moves. It's an action-oriented way of life, which the managerial personality is at home with. Clearly, it's an intuitive management style. And since planning makes managers a bit more analytical, a bit more deliberate, they risk becoming less intuitive, thus less comfortable. Planning forces managers to strap on only one gun. It limits them to just three silver bullets—to no longer shooting at anything that moves, but instead aiming at just one or two carefully selected targets. There's no more box load of ammo, no more two guns blazing every day all day long—just more aiming, more focus, more "per plan."

Managers look upon this as a constraint. And it is a constraint. But it's one of those things they just have to accept. If they wish to benefit from planning, they have to modify their management style to be somewhat more focused. (Fortunately for you, dear reader, I'll stop just short of saying they have to "bite the bullet" to overcome this hurdle to planning.)

Examining Weaknesses—A Painful Process

The difficulty of self-examination is the last hurdle to planning. During planning sessions, managers conduct a situation analysis, addressing the question, "Where are we today?" They look inside the organization for strengths and weaknesses, and outside for opportunities and threats.

Looking inside the organization for internal strengths is a lot of fun. Managers ask what they're good at, talk about those factors, and proudly list them in writing. Then they get to the flip side of that coin and ask, "what are the things we're not so good at? What are our internal weaknesses?"

They have to uncover any weaknesses in functional areas or talents they may lack. They may have to identify the fact that they are in an unfavorable position in the marketplace compared to the competition or that the quality of service is not up to par. They may develop a list of a half dozen or more items that have been identified as internal weaknesses. And here it's tough to open up.

But they must. If managers are to achieve the benefits of planning, they'll have to accurately identify their weaknesses. Only then can they develop strategies to counter those weaknesses. That means they must openly and honestly discuss those weaknesses.

I facilitated a strategic planning retreat for a company in Palm Springs, California. On the morning of the first day, after listing internal strengths, we were developing internal weaknesses. It was a tough session. One significant weakness that did not come out was the fact that there was a delegation problem at the very top of the company—a problem with the president. Other executives in the room merely hinted at it, but no one came right out and said it.

Finally it came out—not during the morning session, but later that evening at dinner. The group had enjoyed a short joke-telling session over cocktail hour. As they loosened up over a steak dinner and a bottle of wine, the executives began kidding each other, first in jest and later in "half-truth." Pretty soon the group was wide open in telling the president about his delegation problem. The next morning we walked back into the conference room and added, "President has delegation problem" to our list of weaknesses. And it was the president himself who reminded us to add the weakness.

20

Getting Ready for Strategic Planning

Following management's decision to proceed with strategic planning, you must prepare people in your organization for the task—most notably, those who will play a role on the planning team. An educational workshop not only educates but builds enthusiasm among members of the planning team. For in the workshop, participants work on an actual case and develop a "mini" strategic plan. And while working on that case, participants extend their thinking into their own organization. Thus the workshop builds enthusiasm for applying the planning process to the participants' own organizations.

It's fair to say that you must not only educate and stimulate the planning team members but also *guide their expectations.* That is, you must make them aware that planning is not the cure for all ills. It won't turn dark into light, night into day, or bad into good. Nor will it automatically make them all better managers. Rather, it will provide a format in which to examine key issues, an examination that hopefully (depending on their decision-making ability) will lead to the right strategic decisions.

I'm reminded of a story regarding another consultant, who received a call from an executive in the Pacific Northwest. The executive said, "Don, I need your help. I'd like you to come up here to work with our managers in putting together a strategic plan for our organization." Don replied that he'd be happy to assist and went on to ask the executive a few questions.

After ten minutes, Don realized that the man's organization was about three-eighths of an inch away from a Chapter 11 bankruptcy filing. "I want you to appreciate the fact that I'm not the right person to help you," Don said. "I think you need something very different from a strategic plan, thus a different type of talent." He suggested an attorney.

Naturally, the caller was disappointed. He thanked Don for his time and was about to hang up. But Don inserted one more question: "Tell me, why didn't you call me two years ago?"

"Because two years ago we didn't need a strategic plan," the executive replied.

Sad, but true. Here's a case of an individual expecting too much from the planning process. So be realistic about your expectations of planning—or any other management tool, for that matter.

The final step in getting ready for strategic planning is the "plan to plan"—the nuts and bolts, the mechanics. The schedule: When and where? The definition of roles: Who makes arrangements for hotel, meeting room, meals, and supplies? Who facilitates the sessions, leads the discussions, directs the process? Who works from the dozens of large pieces of paper to develop the written plan?

And how about the agenda for the sessions? What information is required for the sessions? market surveys? financials? prior years' plans?

And who will furnish copies of all this information to the members of the planning team? And is it the kind of information the team members can get at the session, or will they need it a couple of weeks beforehand so they can read it, understand it, and be prepared to discuss it?

With these preliminary decisions out of the way, you're ready to begin work on the strategic plan.

21

Gathering the Necessary Information

Too often, management teams begin their strategy sessions without first having done their homework. Twenty minutes or so before their first session, they consider, "How should I prepare for this meeting?" And so they end up looking around their desk and gathering up this, this, and that. Little preparation leads to little strategic thinking.

Information Required

To ensure that the planning team arrives at the strategy sessions with the information necessary to develop a viable strategic plan, you've got to give some thought to the information they'll need. That's the purpose of the Information Required form (see Figure 21-1).

Here's how you use it. You hold a short meeting with the members of the planning team about a month to six weeks prior to the first strategy session. At that meeting, the team identifies the information it'll require during its strategy sessions. It also identifies the person who

Figure 21-1. The information required form.

INFORMATION REQUIRED		
What?	Who?	When? Before or During

already has that information or can most easily obtain it. Finally, it decides whether that individual should simply have the information tucked into a briefcase for use during the planning sessions or if he should communicate it to each member of the planning team before the sessions.

The planners needn't start from scratch in thinking about the information they'll need. They can benefit from the use of a checklist. Here's a sample:

Pre-Planning Information

    I. History of the organization

   II. Organization chart

  III. Financial statements
     A. Balance sheet
     B. Income statement
     C. One-year budget

  IV. Published (internally) marketing tools
     A. Brochures
     B. Ads
     C. Publicity releases
     D. Sales tools
     E. Other

   V. Published (externally) market information
     A. Trends of significance
     B. Surveys
     C. Growth rates
     D. Other

  VI. Revenue breakdown by type of product (or service) and by market segment

 VII. Analysis of competition

VIII. List of new projects, products, and processes

  IX. Facilities information (key issues—capacity, information, room for expansion, etc.)

   X. Personnel information (again, key issues—motivation, recruiting problems, etc.)

Naturally, this entire list isn't applicable to every organization. So use it as a guide. Add or subtract as appropriate to your needs. Just be sure that your planners all share a common base of information when preparing for your strategy sessions.

Communicating the Information

It's important to consider how you'll communicate the information which the individual members of your team have gathered. Some information you'll simply want available "on the spot." This might include financial ratios, an annual report, or sales by region. It's sufficient to have someone tuck the information into a briefcase, bring it to the strategy sessions, and present it if and when it's required.

Other types of information should be thought about in advance so that the planners can be ready to discuss them intelligently. Examples include a customer profile, a market survey, or an analysis of profit by category of product or service. Here, communicating the information some time before the planning sessions is beneficial.

It may help to use an information-sharing meeting during which those responsible for communicating information actually make stand-up presentations to the entire planning team. Such meetings encourage the planners to do a better job on both gathering and communicating the required information; in addition, since all are committed to a formal presentation on the same date, they're more diligent about meeting their deadline.

Value/Philosophies Choices Form

Another useful tool for information gathering is the Value/Philosophies Choices form, intended to highlight issues with which you must deal at the planning sessions, issues related to the organization's values and its basic philosophies.

The Value/Philosophies Choices form consists of eighteen examples of contrasting values or philosophies (see Figure 21-2).

Each member of the planning team is asked to first place an "X" on each line where his or her own value lies, that is, where he or she would prefer that the organization operate.

Next, team members place an "O" on each line indicating where they believe the organization actually operates. When an individual is finished with the form,

Figure 21-2. Sampling from value/philosophies choices form.

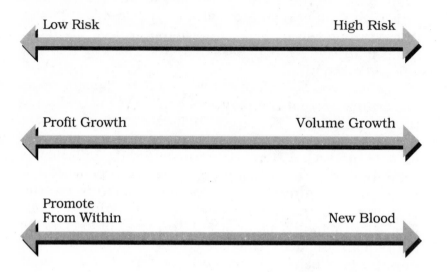

Low Risk   High Risk

Profit Growth   Volume Growth

Promote
From Within   New Blood

each line will have an "X" and an "O" marked somewhere on it.

Each member of the planning team then sends the
completed form (or a copy of it) anonymously to whomever will facilitate the strategic planning sessions. The
facilitator then copies *all* of the X's and O's onto a blank
Values/Philosophies Choices form and evaluates the results.

Sometimes the facilitator discovers that the managers on the planning team are split on whether they
should have a centralized or a decentralized organization
(see Figure 21-3).

And sometimes he or she discovers that the team is
in agreement that diversity is desirable, but that it per-
ceives that the organization's market is concentrated
rather than diverse (see Figure 21-4).

And sometimes the planning team members agree
on wanting participatory management, but are split on
whether management is actually participative or authoritative (see Figure 21-5).

Figure 21-3. Possible choices on centralization axis.

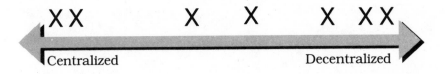

Figure 21-4. Possible choices on diversification axis.

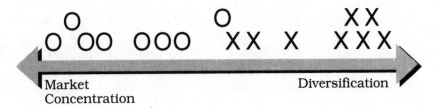

Figure 21-5. Possible choices on participation axis.

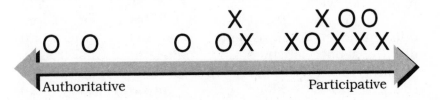

After compiling the forms, the facilitator makes copies for all of the planning team members. Then, at the opening of the strategy sessions, the facilitator begins with a presentation of the findings. And from time to time during the strategy discussions—particularly while discussing internal strengths and weaknesses—he or she may refer to the information provided through use of the Value/Philosophies form.

How About Input From Employees?

On occasion, a client asks us for advice on soliciting pre-planning information from employees other than those on the planning team. And we certainly encourage their doing so. In fact, we believe that getting others involved in the gathering of pre-planning information paves the way for more successful implementation of the resultant strategies.

Involving other employees is easy. Each manager on the planning team can simply include the input from others in his or her department on the Information Required form, for example, or distribute additional copies of the Value/Philosophies Choices form. Or an additional form customized to the specific needs of the individual organization can be developed.

There are three items to consider, however. First, whenever distributing forms to individuals, you should build into your process a method for maintaining the anonymity of each person. You'll obtain more candid—thus more valuable—comments, and more motivated employees as well.

Second, you may wish to compile the responses from different levels of management separately. You can handle this separation by simply coding the forms. It's fascinating to see, and useful to understand, how different the perceptions can be between top and middle management. But be sure you make it known to all that you're maintaining such separation.

Last, be sure to provide timely feedback to all who offer information. If a person gives you an opinion, you owe that person an answer—not that your planning team need necessarily build a specific strategy around that idea. You simply must assure your respondents that their ideas were given consideration. Remember, asking for input implies the promise of feedback. That's only fair.

22

Resources Required for Planning

The resources required for strategic planning include people, place, and time.

The Planning Team

Let's first discuss the most important of these resources—the people. The people on the planning team consist primarily of the company's key executives, for two reasons. First, they are the individuals who have the knowledge of important issues and can best put together the strategies for the organization.

They're also there because their commitment is necessary to the successful implementation of the strategic plan. And what better way to build their commitment than to involve them in the development of the plan?

There can also be another category of individual on the planning team—an "outsider." An outsider can be there for one of two reasons. First, an outsider may be present to fill a void—to make up for a lack of information among the firm's managers. A bank executive, for example, may join the planning team to fill an information (or talent) void in financial management. Or an advertising executive or marketing consultant may function as a temporary member of the planning team because the insiders are weak in marketing talent. Such outside resource persons may come from various corners of the business world—from the board of directors, or the parent company, or a sister division. Or one may be an outside consultant. All will work if it's the *right* person.

The second reason an outsider might be present is to facilitate the process. This requires someone who is knowledgeable in the area of strategic planning and who is skilled in handling the personal dynamics of the planning team.

One precaution regarding the use of any outside person for your strategic planning sessions: Regardless of the reason an outside person is present, please remember, and make sure that person remembers, he or she is just visiting. The plan isn't the consultant's; it's yours. The plan belongs to the people inside the organization. Outsiders can suggest; they can counsel; they can ask the right questions. But they can not make the strategic decisions. That's the job of the insiders.

If any of the insiders walk out of the room saying, "That's a pretty good plan that Ernie put together for us," I can promise you'll have trouble implementing that plan. Your insiders must instead walk out of the room saying, "We did a good job on that plan."

I'm often asked about the maximum number of individuals you should have on the planning team. When the number gets up into the teens, I find the group dynamics to be difficult. I've worked with groups as large as thirty-one people and experienced some difficulty with hearing out all team members. In a very large group, there may be nine people that have something they'd like to say, all at the same time! The person then speaking will be conscious of this and will feel rushed. It's like when you're eating your meal at a restaurant and you see people waiting at the door for an available table.

You become uneasy because you know they're watching you.

Another problem with having a large number of people on the planning team is they generally come from three or four levels within the organization. That's a problem because if not only one's boss but one's boss's boss is in the room, an individual may be reluctant to "open up" about internal strengths and weaknesses. And with three or four levels of managers in the room, top management may likewise be reluctant to share its thoughts.

On the other side, you require a critical mass on the low end. Depending on the business, on the personalities of the people involved, on their relationships, and on just how much they work together on a day-to-day basis, that low end is somewhere around four or five individuals. Below that number, you just don't have critical mass, and the facilitator is very busy keeping the conversation going.

About seven to ten members on a planning team works very nicely. Based on my experience, those are the ideal numbers from a *process* point of view.

More important than the number, however, is who you need in the room. Remember, your planning team should consist of individuals who are both capable of putting together a meaningful strategic plan and responsible for the implementation of the strategies within that plan. Getting the right people in the room is far more important than having a convenient number of individuals.

The Meeting Place

Next let's talk about the hiding place. Note I didn't say "place." I said "hiding place." By all means, get "off-campus" for your planning sessions. Go away to someplace where the phone will not ring. Where people will not knock on the door and ask you to return to your office "just for a moment" to stomp out a brushfire or two. Where the urgencies of the hour will not demand that you focus on day-to-day tasks.

Some years ago, I worked with a small manufacturing company in Southern California. The president of the company said to me, "Bill, you know we're tight on cash. Let's try to keep our planning costs as low as possible. Couldn't we hold our planning sessions here in our own conference room?" I was about to say, "No, because . . . ." when the president added, "You know there's a holiday weekend coming up, and we can spend the three days meeting right here in our conference room. Surely, we won't be interrupted. Our employees are all off for the weekend. Nobody will call us. And the mail-man won't deliver mail. We will be uninterrupted, I promise."

So I agreed.

And the president was right. It worked. It worked for twenty minutes. At twenty minutes after eight on the first morning of our meeting, the marketing manager turned to the vice-president and said, "Dave, I'm not sure you're right on that point. In fact, I just got a letter from our sales rep in Dallas. He had some figures on this very issue. His letter is sitting in my office. Why don't you pour yourself a cup of coffee while I get the letter? I'll be right back." And out the door went the marketing manager.

Dave was about to sip his second cup of coffee when I decided I'd better go find our marketing manager. Down the hall I went, entered Bob's office to discover he had emptied one file cabinet drawer onto his desk. He was well into the second drawer, looking for the letter from the sales guy in Dallas. I suggested he return to the conference room without the letter. He replied, "But I'm trying to make a point with Dave." I asked if he remembered the letter pretty well. He said, "Yes." So I said, "Come on back to the conference room and tell us what-ever you remember about the letter."

The point is: Don't fall into the trap. Get "off-campus." Find a hiding place.

Allocating the Necessary Time

Time is the third resource to be dedicated to the planning process. The obvious time is that required for the actual planning sessions. But don't forget the less obvious time—the "get-ready time" preceding and the "homework time" following the meetings.

It requires about three full days of meetings—the "obvious time"—for the planning team to develop its strategic plan. That includes a day each for situation analysis, objective setting, and developing strategy.

Those three days can be devoted to the process in one of two ways—either a series of meetings spaced about two weeks apart or a "long weekend"—a three-day, off-site planning "retreat."

Both methods have their advantages. The "series of meetings" method offers the opportunity for reflective thinking. Planning team members get the chance to sleep on issues discussed in earlier sessions and return to the later meetings with a "fresh" approach. Two weeks between meetings works well.

Also, the series of meetings offers the chance to seek out resources helpful to later meetings—reports, data, people (or a letter from the sales guy in Dallas).

The series of meetings is generally less expensive. If most of the members on the planning team are local, working a normal workday and going home each evening saves hotel and meal expenses.

The "long weekend" planning retreat also has advantages. For one, it's a whole lot easier on travel schedules. If some of the planners are coming from out of town, you'll get them in for a three-day retreat much more easily than for a series of one-day meetings spaced two weeks apart.

Also, the "long weekend" retreat is a dedicated session. For three days or so, the planning team eats, breathes, and sleeps the strategic plan. It's intense. Team members "get up to speed" just once, on the start of the first day, rather than the start of each day.

And the "long weekend" offers the chance for valuable informal discussions—during dinner, over drinks, before and after meetings. The cross-fertilization of ideas coming from small informal groups during "break times" is most valuable. And living together for three days encourages teambuilding, a great by-product of the planning process.

Also, the "long weekend" retreat "big deals" the process just a bit. It makes a statement about management's commitment to the strategic plan.

One more advantage to the three-day retreat: It's generally farther away from the office and from interruptions. Planning team members can't "swing by the office just for a minute."

23
Planning Assumptions

As part of their planning process, most management teams develop a set of planning assumptions.

Assumptions are necessary because you can't afford to spend the time to develop a different plan for every possible combination of future events. Certainly, you can't afford to build a strategic plan that accounts for 5 percent inflation next year, another strategic plan for 8 percent inflation next year, and a third strategic plan for 9.5 percent inflation next year. It's simply more practical to develop a strategic plan assuming an inflation rate of 7 percent perhaps. Or a range of inflation, 6 percent to 8 percent, for example.

Planners must also develop a reasonable set of assumptions on demographics, on the probability of another war in the Middle East, or on any other relevant contingency over the life of the plan. You see, these assumptions limit the scope of the planning horizon and thus make the planning process more feasible.

You have to review your assumptions on a periodic basis to make sure they're valid.

But when, during the planning process, does the management team develop its assumptions? You have two choices. First, the team can decide before its planning sessions, prior to situation analysis, which specific assumptions it requires and then go about developing those assumptions.

Organizations which need to consolidate a number of strategic plans—those of its divisions or subsidiaries, perhaps—must develop their assumptions prior to the planning sessions. That will assure that each division or subsidiary is using the same set of assumptions. If they don't set assumptions first, they may find one division's plan assumes a 6 percent inflation factor and another division's, 7.5 percent. And the corporation will have a heck of a time consolidating the two plans.

As a second choice, the management team can wait until its planning sessions and there develop its assumptions. If it does wait to develop its assumptions during the process, the team will typically do so while creating its objectives.

Consider this example: When you get to that point in the process when you ask, "What objectives would we like to set?" someone might suggest you set an objective to measure increased sales revenue. The person may further suggest that since business is pretty good, the company can aim for a 20 percent sales increase next year. A second person might ask, "Do you mean 20 percent growth before or after inflation? That is, does the 20 percent growth figure you suggest include an inflation factor or doesn't it?" The first person might well respond, "Oh, I guess I'm including inflation when I propose 20 percent." Someone may then ask, "Well, how much inflation are you assuming?" And then, you need an assumption.

24

Key Success Factors

On the first morning of company strategy sessions, I ask the planning team an important question. On a flip-chart easel, I write:

For our organization to be successful, we *must* be good at which specific activities?

1. _____
2. _____
3. _____

Then, I challenge the group to provide two or three answers (but no more) to that question.

I ask the people in the room to first spend a few moments thinking about the question and writing their individual answers. Then I have them read their answers aloud. We discuss any differences of opinion and finally arrive at a consensus. We record those final answers on the flip-chart easel and entitle the list "Key Success Factors."

In this exercise, we've provided a short list of "activities we've got to be good at." And that's important. For we're about to do our situation analysis (see Chapter 25). Within that situation analysis, we'll first compile lists of internal strengths and internal weaknesses, including the very important factors and excluding the very unimportant ones. As a client in Colorado once put it, "We don't want to spend our valuable time discussing the color of the stripes in the parking lot."

He's right. You want to use your time discussing those factors most important to your success—your key success factors.

It's important to limit the list of key success factors to two, or at most three. Here's why.

In creating lists of "things we've got to be good at," management teams frequently include six or eight factors. Typically, they'll list "understanding the customer," "producing a low-cost product," "managing expenses," "hiring good people," and "developing innovative marketing programs."

The lists are certainly complete. Too complete! They're so all-inclusive, they're not much more than "apple pie and motherhood." And they certainly don't imply focus.

But focus is exactly what's required for success— focus on the most important things, on two or three (no more) key success factors. In any business, there are two or three factors which are the primary determinants of success. If the firm's management team is good at those factors and just mediocre at everything else, the company will be successful. Yes, you read it right, *mediocre* at everything else.

Here's an example. In the real estate development industry, land acquisition and liquidity are the two key success factors. If every other factor concerning the business of the development company is just average, but the land acquired has the right location and the firm maintains adequate liquidity, the company will do well. Not that the developer shouldn't attempt to deliver a well-constructed product with good financing. But nothing is a greater determinant of success than having or not having the right piece of land and remaining in a liquid position.

Knowing the importance of land acquisition to his

company's success, the chairman of one real estate development company instructed his managers, "Before you commit to the purchase of any piece of land, I want to walk on it." Another real estate development company executive explained, "The real estate business is really the land investment business. Fortunately, if the developer selects the wrong piece of land, he has an out. He can put a building on the land to get rid of it."

In the computer software market, the key success factors are establishing efficient channels of distribution and providing after-sales support. Too much concern about writing "efficient code" may be a technical nicety, but from a competitive point of view, it's probably a waste of resources.

In the management consulting business, the key success factors are communicating with executive decision makers and satisfying client needs. Too much concern about controlling expenses is focusing on the wrong thing.

In the airline business, the name of the game is to fill planes with passengers. Improving food and beverage quality and efficient handling of baggage are interesting things to work on, but they don't make or break an airline. Keeping planes full does.

Be sure you're aware of the key success factors in your business. Then make sure you're good at those factors. And don't spend a bunch of resources getting too good at a lot of things that aren't as important.

25

Situation Analysis

Each of the critical questions ("Where are we today?" "Where do we wish to arrive, and when?" and "How do we get from here to there?") is addressed during a specific step in the planning process. Let's discuss the first of those questions, "Where are we today?" This question is dealt with during the planning process step called *situation analysis.*

Situation Analysis—What It Includes

Situation analysis requires that we look in two directions—both inside and outside the organization.

When examining the company's internal factors, we develop two lists, "Internal Strengths" and "Internal Weaknesses." We arrive at those two lists through a critical analysis of the entire firm. We look at management—its leadership, its planning, its development of personnel, its delegation of responsibility and authority.

We examine each of the functional areas in the organization, like marketing and sales, product and service development, production and inventory control, finance and accounting.

We look at the organization's resources, including

financial resources, facilities, employees, and information.

When compiling your list of internal weaknesses, be careful. Occasionally planning teams, in attempting to list internal weaknesses, include not weaknesses, but symptoms of weaknesses, such as "We have a low market share" or "Our sales are flat" or "Our company is not growing." None of those statements refers to a weakness. Each describes a symptom of a weakness.

To cut through the symptom and discover the weakness itself, ask "Why?" If you can come up with an answer to the "Why?" question, then the answer is probably a whole lot closer to the actual weakness than the original symptom statement.

And watch for this: In an internal analysis, you'll often have an item that appears, in different words, on both your strengths and weaknesses lists—"excess capacity in engineering," as an example.

Excess capacity in engineering has a positive aspect. It represents an available resource, an expertise in plentiful supply. Thus it belongs on the "strengths" list. But under-utilization of the engineering department may well come up on the "weaknesses" list. There, from a financial point of view, it represents the fact that the asset is being paid for but not fully used. Both statements are right; they simply represent different points of view. The first takes the capability point of view—that's the strength. The other takes the financial point of view—underutilization of the asset—that's the weakness.

The Macro- and Micro-Environments

When you're finished with the internal analysis, you can turn your attention toward the external analysis and develop two additional lists, "External Opportunities" and "External Threats."

Where do you look for external opportunities and

threats? You look first in a world called the macro-environment (see Figure 25-1). The macro-environment is a big, broad place. It's the entire world. It's the world at large, all things, as somehow related to your organization.

Issues in the macro-environment are not specific to your company. They're not even specific to your industry.

Figure 25-1. The macro- and micro-environments.

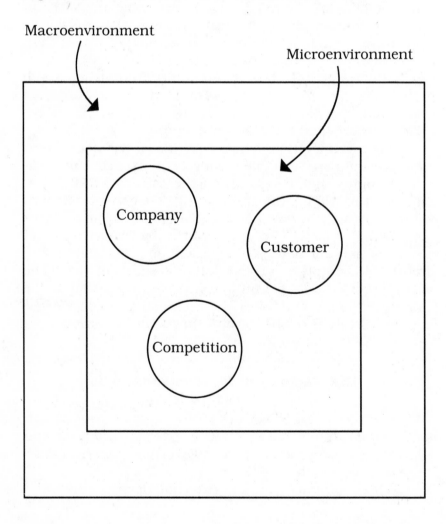

But you care about them because they affect you. They include things like economic conditions. Economic conditions are not specific to any one industry. Rather, economic conditions have an impact on all companies. The economy, then, is a macro-environmental issue.

Government regulations and politics similarly are macro-environmental issues, as are consumer attitudes. Demographic data—people moving into or out of regional areas, the aging of the population, women's changing role in the work force—again are not industry-specific. These issues affect all industries. They are macro-environmental factors.

After looking at the macro-environmental factors, you consider the micro-environment—the world a whole lot closer to home. It's the world in which your organization, its customers, its suppliers, its labor force, and its competitors function. It's the industry and the marketplace in which you participate.

The micro-environment includes the industries, or segments of industries, to which your customers belong, the reasons why your customers buy your products or services, and the reasons why some prospective customers don't. Supplier relationships, the labor market— all of these are micro-environmental factors, factors specific to your industry.

One micro-environmental factor that's easy to overlook is the technology that relates your firm to its customers. When the first oil crisis occurred in October 1973, it took a lot of companies by surprise. Included among the surprised organizations were those in the fast-food franchise business. For many years, the fast-food franchisers believed that the technology relating their business to their customers was their ability to fry french fries in hot oil, when in reality, a more significant link to their customers was the internal combustion engine. People had to drive their automobiles to buy the American meal—hamburger, fries, and a Coke. And during the oil crisis, Americans needed a far better reason to use a gallon of gasoline.

Analyzing the Competition

No look at the external environment is complete without an analysis of the competition. The competitive analysis includes an examination of the market segments served by both your company and the competition—your market share versus theirs, marketing mix including product and service quality, pricing, and distribution. You need a thorough examination of competitor strengths and weaknesses.

Competitor strengths and weaknesses are an important element in the situation analysis because a competitor strength translates into an external threat for your company, and a competitor weakness translates into an external opportunity for your company.

Here's something to watch for in compiling lists of external opportunities and threats. Technological innovation is viewed by some companies as an opportunity and by other companies as a threat.

The difference is in the relative positions of the companies writing the two statements. The firm viewing technological innovation as an opportunity is at the cutting edge of its industry. The organization viewing technological innovation as a threat is a laggard or a "me too" producer.

That's interesting. It means that if we take an issue, such as technological innovation, we don't automatically know if that issue should go on an opportunity list or a threat list. It depends upon the internal position of the organization.

The same is true for other issues such as "increasing demand for product quality," "high interest rates," and "demand for higher level of service."

Once more, be careful. In attempting to list opportunities, many planning teams mistakenly include a strategy or two. And it's no surprise, for opportunities and strategies are easily confused. Remember this— opportunities are outside the walls of the business, things that are there for you to take advantage of if you so choose. They're there absolutely independent of the existence of your organization.

And since opportunities are independent of your firm's existence, they describe no action by your firm. So opportunity statements have no action verbs. They don't say, "Let's spin off into the foreign commercial market." Or "Let's develop a new product line for the mid-price market." In those cases, you're really writing strategies.

If you recognize a market demand in the foreign commercial market, then write an opportunity statement that says exactly that. Sure, you'll also develop strategies, but at a later step in the planning process. During the situation analysis, you're developing only four lists: internal strengths, internal weaknesses, external opportunities and external threats.

26

The Bell-Shaped Curve

On a scale of 1 to 10, most neckties cost about 5.5. Sure, you can buy some very fine hand-sewn silk neckties whose prices would score a 9 or 10. And you can score a 1 or 2 by shopping for a necktie in a discount department store. But if you took all the prices of all the neckties for sale and ranked them on a scale of 1 to 10, you'd find their prices clustered around 5.5.

And on a scale of 1 to 10, most adult American males are 5.5 tall. Sure, the heights of the Boston Celtics score a 9.5, and some very short men score 1 or 2. But on a scale of 1 to 10, the vast majority of them center around 5.5.

This "bell-shaped curve" is a natural phenomenon (see Figure 26-1). It applies with such frequency that it's called the "normal distribution." It works not only for neckties and for men's heights, but also for the acceleration of automobiles, the time required to shine your shoes, and the annual rainfall in your hometown.

And it works in the world of business, too. Consider an activity for which your organization might score itself against its competitors—marketing, for example. A few firms are excellent at marketing; IBM comes to mind immediately. IBM scores a 9 or 10 in marketing. And some companies are terrible at marketing—like many of the organizations that go broke each year. They score a 1 or 2.

Figure 26-1. The bell-shaped curve.

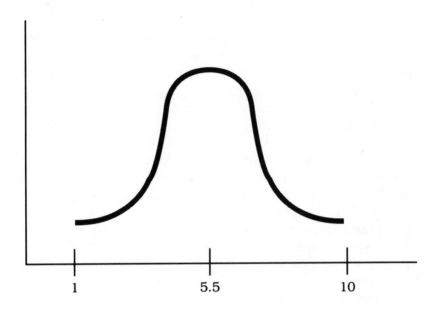

Most firms, however, are just about as good at marketing as a whole bunch of their competitors. On a scale of 1 to 10, they score about 5 or 6. Here too, the bell-shaped curve works.

It works too for cost of manufacturing, for product development, and for financial capacity. For each of those factors, almost everyone in the industry falls near the middle of the curve—about 5.5—while a few score very high and a few score very low.

The bell-shaped curve is particularly useful when you're considering organizational strengths and weaknesses because it helps you view those strengths and weaknesses in comparison to your competition. And that's important. It isn't enough to say "We're good" (at marketing, for example). You must be able to say, "We're significantly better at marketing than our competitors are."

Think about each suggested strength and weakness in comparison with your competitors. How do you score?

Right there in the middle of the pack—a 4, 5, 6, or 7
with all the rest? Or do you score a 1, 2, or 3? In financial
management, perhaps? If so, you've just identified a competitive weakness, something you can work to correct.

Go on to score the next issue. Marketing, perhaps.
How do you score? About 8 or 9? Good. You've identified
a competitive strength. The trick, of course, is to develop
strategies that employ those strengths to your advantage.

An interesting example of an organization building
on internal strengths comes from a small electronics
instrumentation manufacturer on the West Coast. The
company, formed by two talented engineers, works in
the field of process instrumentation. The company is
very good at going out into the factories of the nation,
finding out what a particular process is all about, identifying specific measurement problems, wrapping its arms
around those problems, and inventing solutions. This
little company focuses on those tougher problems and
manages to carve out a nice little niche for itself in an
otherwise very competitive marketplace.

Use the bell-shaped curve to identify your company's
strengths and weaknesses as compared with your competition. Then be sure the strategies you develop build
on your strengths and correct your weaknesses.

27

Mission Statement

Between the situation analysis and objective-setting sessions, the planning team develops its mission statement, a short, succinct statement declaring what business you're in and who your customer is. By offering this focus, it provides direction for the future and lays the groundwork for the objectives and strategies to follow.

In 1960, Theodore Levitt wrote a significant article in the *Harvard Business Review*. In his article, "Marketing Myopia," Levitt criticized American business managers who, he claimed, define their business from the inside out. That is, American business managers focus on the products and services they provide, the nuts and bolts of their business. And this, suggested Levitt, is a serious mistake.

To illustrate his point, Levitt claimed that the railroad industry caused its own decline by insisting that "we're in the railroad business." That statement led the railroad companies to think in terms of great hunks of iron and steel, rights-of-way a quarter of a mile wide across the United States, and large quantities of coal shipped across the Great Lakes. As they thought in terms of these physical factors and insisted, "We're in the railroad business," they missed opportunities to participate in the growth segments of the transportation industry—in automobiles, trucks, and airplanes.

According to Levitt, if the railroad companies had said, "We're in the *transportation* business," they might have fared much better. How come?

Because the railroad industry's customers don't care about the iron and the steel. They don't care about rights-of-way across the country. They don't care about great quantities of coal. They simply care about moving people and things from one place to another. The market need that the railroads serve is transportation, not railroading.

Certainly, Levitt has a point. But there's another point, too. The railroad industry happens to own the rights-of-way across the United States. They happen to own the tracks. They happen to own the iron and steel. All their assets have to do with the railroad industry. There are, after all, two sides to this story.

A mission statement incorporates both points of view: an inside-out description of what you do—the product or service you supply and the functional activities you perform inside the walls of your company—and the market-sided point of view—"Who buys it, and why?"

For example:

> Clayton Instruments, Inc., designs and manufactures highly reliable monitoring equipment to meet harsh or unusual environments within the process industries.

Consider the first half of Clayton's mission statement:

> Clayton Instruments, Inc., designs and manufactures highly reliable monitoring equipment. . . .

This part of the statement lists the functional activities performed: "designs and manufactures." And it describes the products that Clayton ships out the back door: "highly reliable monitoring equipment."

Consider the second half of Clayton's mission statement:

to meet harsh or unusual environments within
the process industries.

This part describes the "Who buys it and why?" It's the market-sided definition of Clayton's business. It establishes a position for the firm and, by so doing, suggests direction for the future.

A well-developed mission statement is broad enough to allow for the diversity management intends. It also provides the focus to describe accurately what products and services the company offers.

Continuing with our Clayton Instruments example, though the company currently manufactures temperature and pressure monitors only, its mission statement describes the firm's products more broadly. It speaks of "monitoring equipment." This leaves room for the company's introduction of equipment other than temperature and pressure monitors. Thus the mission statement allows room for product expansion.

At the same time, the mission statement provides focus. It identifies the company's market as the process industries. It specifically targets applications in "harsh or unusual environments."

Also, the word "monitoring" provides additional focus. Clayton Instruments does not manufacture data logging equipment. It does not manufacture control equipment. The company manufactures monitoring equipment and consciously eliminates other products through its mission statement. Presumably, the company's executives have explored Clayton's position in the industry and concluded that its expertise is in monitoring equipment.

Expect very little change in your mission statement from year to year. Change in your mission statement is evolutionary rather than revolutionary. That's because the mission statement presents a foundation for what the company is, what it does, for whom, and why. As the foundation of your business—your link to your customers—you wouldn't want it to change very much from year to year.

Think of your mission statement as you do the Constitution of the United States. You *can* change the Constitution. But you can't change it much. And you can't change it fast. Same with your mission statement.

A number of companies add one more item to their mission statement—a reference to "earning a profit" or "providing a return on stockholder equity."

This gives the mission statement a secondary purpose. Its primary purpose, of course, is to relate the organization to its market. Adding "for a profit" to the mission statement relates the company to its stockholders. This can be helpful in getting the board of directors to approve the strategic plan of which the mission statement is a part.

This point relates to a second school of thought regarding the mission statement. This point of view advocates a statement that addresses not just the relationship with the customer, but a number of other relationships as well—those with the stockholders, the employees, the community, the free enterprise system.

While I certainly agree that each of those relationships is important, I feel that just one of them—the relationship with the customer—is more important than the others. For if the organization doesn't maintain its relationship with its customer, all its other relationships would certainly be academic. The relationship with the customer is clearly the foundation for the enterprise.

Let's suppose that the management team decides to develop a short, succinct mission statement—one describing its relationship with its customers only. But the management team also feels that a number of other relationships—with employees and suppliers perhaps—are important as well. Where in the strategic plan do they document those relationships?

The team has a couple of choices. First, it can develop

a section of the plan called "management philosophy" in which it discusses philosophies, values, culture, and relationships. Or, in the plan's Introduction, it can discuss these same issues. More on this point later when we examine the outline of the strategic plan (see Chapter 37).

28

Categories of Objectives

In addressing strategic planning's second key question—
"Where do we wish to arrive, and when?"—your management team will develop a set of quantified objectives.
When developing objectives for your organization, you've
got six categories to consider:

1. Financial
2. Marketing/sales
3. Products/services
4. Operations
5. Human resources
6. Community

Within each of these six categories, you can select
from a number of specific measurements for each objective. For example, you can set your financial objective
to measure profitability in any of its various flavors, such
as gross profit, operating profit, or net profit, either before
or after tax. Or you can write your financial objective in
terms of return on assets, return on investment, or cash
on hand.

You might write your marketing or sales objective in

terms of sales volume, sales growth rate, market share, or number of market segments effectively served.

Similarly, you might define your products and services objective as quality of products and services, introduction of new products and services, or customer satisfaction. And your operational objective might measure efficiency, productivity, or cost reduction.

Your objective dealing with human resources—the people side of the business—can measure employee benefits, employee satisfaction, employee training, or employee turnover. Finally, your social objective—your non-economic or community-related objective—might deal with avoiding pollution of air and water, establishing equal opportunity employment, or being a good corporate citizen.

Prioritizing Your Objectives

The order in which we've listed the categories of objectives is not arbitrary. This order, beginning with financial and ending with community, is referred to as the *hierarchy of objectives.* It's the order of priority that managers generally assign to their objectives, the order in which they care about things.

When you get to the part of the planning process where you're ready to set your objectives, the first suggestion you usually hear is, "Let's make a profit." Even the not-for-profit institutions—governmental, educational, charitable—jump to develop their financial objective first. Like their for-profit cousins, they too have financial needs and constraints. And their financial needs are first on the minds of management when setting objectives.

If the financial objective is so important, how can management attain that objective? In the jargon of for-profit firms, "How can we make a buck?"

The way you do it is to sell something to somebody.

All businesses must exchange a product or a service for money. And since it's selling something that produces a profit, the marketing or sales objective must support the financial objective.

Next you need a product or service to sell. That product or service objective supports the marketing/sales objective, just as the marketing/sales objective supports the financial objective.

Operationally, you have to build your product or deliver your service. And it takes people to run the operation. So we evolve the hierarchy.

But be careful. Don't take the hierarchy too seriously. Don't end up with all of your objectives in the top two categories—finance and marketing. If you do, you'll have a problem.

When you communicate your completed plan to the people in your organization and ask them for help in implementing the plan, they'll take a long, hard look at your objectives. If your objectives focus only on profit and sales, your employees will wonder about your plan. Because the people outside of the executive planning group care a whole lot more about the categories near the middle and bottom of the list than about those near the top. That's simply a fact of life. After you get a couple of levels down from the top of the organization, you find a lot less interest in the financial and marketing objectives and a lot more interest in operations and in people. So they'll wonder, "What's in it for me?" If they ask that question out loud, you've got a problem. If they ask it silently, you've got an even more serious problem.

Don't forget—to accomplish your objectives, you'll need the help of all the people in your organization. So balance your objective list. Consider including objectives in each of the six categories. Not that you must necessarily have an objective in each category. But at least consider each. Try to develop a balanced list of objectives so you'll gain the commitment of employees who might otherwise ask, "What's in it for me?"

If you'll benefit from developing more than one objective in a particular category, do it. For example, you may write an objective for total sales, and another for sales of a particular product line or sales to a specific market segment.

Limiting Your Objectives

Be careful not to set too many objectives. If you do, you'll lose focus. You won't be able to use your objectives in managing day-to-day. Consider this: If you can't memorize your objectives, you've probably got too many. For the memories of most of us, six is about the limit.

A few years ago, I worked with a high-tech manufacturing company in Los Angeles. On the second day of that company's planning retreat, the executive management team developed its list of objectives. I opened the objective-setting session with a brief discussion about the categories of objectives, spoke for a few moments on the criteria of objectives, and then asked for suggestions on the first objective to consider.

After a lengthy discussion, the group agreed to a financial objective—pre-tax profit. From there, it moved ahead nicely, developed four or five well-quantified, challenging (yet achievable) objectives. So far, so good. But the group kept going. There were another three or four suggested objectives still "alive." I stood up and gave my first little "mini-speech" about the hazards of setting too many objectives.

Just the same, the group continued developing objectives. When it completed writing its eighth objective, I delivered my second mini-speech. My third warning came between the tenth and eleventh.

In all, the group set thirteen objectives. About twice the number it should have. Knowing it couldn't possibly focus on all thirteen, I had the group set priorities among its objectives.

And I'm glad I did. Because within six months, the

company's managers had forgotten about their "C" priority objectives. They were working on all the "A" and a couple of the "B" objectives. But they had spent nearly six months scrambling in an unfocused attempt to accomplish all thirteen. Efficient use of resources? Hardly.

Keep your objectives lists short.

29
Criteria for Objectives

For an objective to be useful, it has to meet certain criteria. First, it must carry a single theme. It should tell you to do one thing only, not two or more. Example: If you decide to increase sales by 15 percent next year, you might write an objective that says exactly that.

But let's imagine you'd also like to increase net profit by 1 percent. Couldn't you write one objective that says, "Do both." Now suppose you write an objective that says, "We will increase sales by 15 percent next year and at the same time, improve net profit by 1 percent." If, by the end of the year, you achieve the 15 percent increase in sales but miss the 1 percent increase in profit, have you made or missed the objective? You could argue it either way. At best, it's ambiguous.

Worse, however, is that the objective does not provide you with guidance in operating your business. Here's why. Imagine that six months after you write your objective calling for 15 percent increase in sales and 1 percent increase in net profit, your sales manager comes running in with the golden opportunity of the month.

"Here's the deal," he says. "We have a grand opportunity to land a really sizable order. And if we get it, this order should be enough to put us over the top—to give us the 15 percent increase in sales we're shooting for."

"Oh yeah," continues your sales manager. "There's some bad news. Since the market is so fiercely competitive, and since our competitors know about this large potential order, we're really going to have to sharpen the pencil to get it. We'll have to shave our price just as far as we can."

So while the "golden opportunity" will go a long way toward achieving the 15 percent increase in sales volume, it will actually detract from the 1 percent increase in profit. Should you go after the big order or not? Your objective statement hasn't provided any guidance in this decision. Why? Because in the same statement, you've bundled together the sales revenue increase and the profitability increase. The objective leaves you to debate which of the two—sales or profit—is the more important.

It's better to pull the objective statement apart and to have one statement that addresses the increase in sales revenue and another that speaks of the increase in profit. Then be sure to do one more thing—*give a different priority to each of the two potentially conflicting objectives.* During your planning sessions, you can argue all you like about whether sales volume or profit is more important. But when your sales manager appears with the his "golden opportunity," you'll know how to respond.

In writing objectives, eliminate the "why" and the "how." If you need to discuss why you're interested in increasing sales by 15 percent next year, you'll have that conversation during the planning sessions. But you won't explain why in your objective statement in an attempt to justify that objective to those who read the plan.

Neither will you describe how you'll accomplish the objective, at least not at this point in the process. You won't write an objective that says, "We'll increase sales volume by 15 percent next year by implementing the following three programs . . ." The answer to "how" is really a strategy, which you'll develop during the next step in the planning process.

Objectives Should Aim at Results

Whenever possible, you should establish results-oriented objectives instead of activities-oriented ones. For example: "We will increase dollar sales by 15 percent next year." That's a results-oriented objective. "We will increase the number of sales calls by 15 percent next year." That's an activities-oriented objective. Obviously, the first is a stronger statement. Whenever possible, write your objectives in terms of a result, rather than an activity.

There are times when you simply can't write a results-oriented objective. If that's the case, write your objective as an activity. "Install the new computer system by the end of the year." "Hire a manager of human resources by June 15th." "Complete the new marketing plan by the third quarter." Each is an activity-oriented objective. Each is used because no result (other than the completion of the activity) can be measured. Each, however, is an exception. Generally, our objectives are results-oriented.

Objectives Should Be Measurable

Objectives must be quantified. When your objective is due for accomplishment, you've got to be able to measure it to figure out whether or not you've succeeded. More important, everyone in the organization has to know how hard to "push to go get it." You've got to quantify your objectives.

Sometimes that's easy, and sometimes it's not, depending on the category of the objective. Financial objectives are the easiest to quantify. After all, the world of finance is a number on a piece of paper. And marketing objectives are usually easy enough to turn into numbers. Certainly you can quantify sales volume. And market share, too, if you can agree on a measurement for industry sales.

But how about something like customer satisfaction? A pretty gray area, isn't it? Some say customer satisfaction is so difficult to quantify that you can't do it. Or can you?

Sure you can! You can count complaints. You can measure defective product. You can count referrals to new accounts. Or repeat business. Or warranty costs. In every case—in all of these suggested ways to measure customer satisfaction—you've taken the same approach. You've decided that customer satisfaction is so difficult to measure that you'll measure something else, something you believe parallels the issue of customer satisfaction.

So when warranty cost gets below 1.5 percent, or when the reorder ratio goes over 75 percent, or when referrals to new accounts reach 25 percent of total billings—then you'll believe that customer satisfaction is where you want it to be. The point is, you quantify your objectives even if you have to "force" your measurement.

Managers often attempt to use market share as a measurable objective. But that's not necessarily a great idea. It's difficult to get agreement on the total market size used in calculating market share. And even if managers can agree on total market size, data on current market size are never available right now. This lack of timely information means you can't use a market share objective to manage your business on a day-to-day basis. For these reasons, market share is most often viewed as an approximate, rather than an exact, measurement. It makes for a poor objective.

But suppose market share is important to your organization, as it is to many. If so, you can write your objective in terms of sales volume. Then you can estimate total market size and put that estimate on your list of planning assumptions. Finally, in an appendix to your plan, you can divide your sales objective by your estimated market size to arrive at your intended market share. That way, you'll have an objective whose measurement (sales volume) is familiar to, and accepted by, those who must accomplish it. And just as important, it's a measurement that's available right now. So you can use it as a day-to-day tool in managing your business.

Objectives Should Be in Harmony

Objectives should be "in concert." It's one thing to write down an objective and say, "Yes, that's fine. I think we can do it. Let's commit to it." Then you go on to the next one and do it again. And again. It's one thing to take each objective one at a time. And it's quite another to write all of your objectives on a piece of paper, tack them up at the front of the room, take a long, hard look at them, and ask, "Can we do this whole bunch of objectives all at the same time?"

For example, let's imagine you're participating in an industry enjoying very fast growth. During your objective-setting session, you decide, because you're in a fast-growth industry, that you'll set an objective that says, "We will build sales revenue by 35 percent next year." You write it down, and you've got your first objective.

A bit later, you remember that cash was pretty tight last year. "Recall that in April we had trouble meeting payroll. Why don't we set an objective that deals with our cash position? Let's set an objective that says, 'During the next year, we'll have, on average, 30 percent more cash in the bank than we had last year.'"

Now you've written a set of objectives calling for growing by 35 percent in one year and at the same time having more cash lying around. But the two are conflicting objectives. Because growth doesn't produce cash. To grow fast, you'll use cash to fuel your way up the growth curve.

My point is obvious—look at your objectives all together to make sure they're in concert. If not, make a choice. Choose among conflicting objectives or modify one or the other. Just so when you're finished with your list of objectives, everyone on your planning team believes you can accomplish them all at the same time.

Objectives Should Be Challenging—But Attainable

Finally, an objective—any objective—should be challenging and, at the same time, attainable. People in your organization should understand that accomplishment of the objective requires that they "reach." But given that reach, they should expect that they can accomplish the objective, that it is achievable.

The analogy I like is that of the basketball hoop. The hoop is ten feet above the floor of the gymnasium. At that ten-foot level, the goal is both challenging and attainable. If the hoop were four feet above the floor of the gymnasium, the game would not be challenging, and the players would not devote much effort to it. Similarly if the hoop were a hundred feet above the floor of the gymnasium, the goal would not be attainable. Again, the players would not devote much effort to the game.

It's your job as a manager to keep your players devoting effort to the game. You must find that "ten-foot level" for each objective. You must make each of your objectives both challenging and attainable.

30
Time Span for an Objective

In deciding how much time you'll need to accomplish a specific objective, you should consider a number of factors. Suppose you're developing an objective to introduce your current product line to a new market and you wonder just how much time you'll need to accomplish that market introduction.

You'll first need to consider the necessary market development activities. Perhaps you'll expand your existing sales force. Or instead, you might hire a new sales force. Most likely, you'll develop an advertising program and a new brochure. The more work required in each of these activities, the more time you'll need to accomplish your objective. And the more your new target market differs from your current market, the more time you'll need, too.

Product or service development is the second factor you'll need to consider in setting a date for fulfilling an objective. Product and service development generally take more time than you initially expect, especially if the new product or service is considerably different from your current products and services in technology, in method of manufacturing (if a product), or in method of delivery (if a service).

You'll need to consider the accounting cycle also. Your entire plan and each objective within it are at the mercy of the accounting cycle. Suppose you discover a way to improve manufacturing efficiency by 2 percent. Then you run out to the factory to try your new idea. You won't know if you were successful until your accounting system cranks out the next factory report. Your planning process works best when you write objectives in conjunction with your fiscal year—or, next best, a fiscal quarter. Because that's when your accounting system provides you with the most information.

Availability of resources is obviously a factor you should consider in setting the time span for your objectives. Suppose you decide to develop a new product for market introduction in six months. And that six-month introduction requires four full-time engineers on the project. Except that you don't have four full-time engineers; you have only two. In that case, you're not going to get the new product in six months. You'll need more time (unless you can hire some more engineers or make use of outside engineering resources).

Finally, the nature of the business is a factor you must also consider in deciding when you can accomplish your objective. Some industries such as software manufacturers—those with very short product life cycles—find shorter-range objectives (a few months, perhaps) appropriate. Other industries—like the forestry industry growing trees for construction material or power utility companies planning substations for future populations—develop objectives with due dates decades away.

31

Objectives of Individuals

Keep in mind that it's individuals in the organization who will make or break the company's objectives. People will either work hard to achieve those company objectives—or they won't. And they're more likely to work hard if you can align the organization's objectives with those of the individuals who will help achieve them.

There was a small Southern California company that had on staff a production manager named Jim, who came to the company soon after it was founded. He was the company's third or fourth employee.

Jim had begun as an electronics technician/assembler. He had worked his way up, and the company had grown, until Jim was now the production manager.

But Jim had one disadvantage. Although he was a valuable and loyal employee and was doing a great job for the company, Jim had never really worked anyplace else in his life. He had come to the company straight out of high school at about age 18. He was now in his mid-twenties. Although he was production manager for the company, he had never seen another factory floor. His experience was terribly narrow.

This was a problem that he was certainly aware of.

The president of the company was also aware of it. Neither Jim nor the president felt comfortable discussing the situation; it never came up.

Then one day, at a board of directors meeting, the president shared with the other directors of the company the problem of Jim's narrow experience.

One of the company's outside directors made an interesting suggestion. That outside director was, at that time, the vice-president of a somewhat larger organization in a similar, though noncompeting, business. The outside director suggested to the president, "Why don't you send Jim to our facility two days a month for a year or so? You have some knowledge, some techniques, that Jim could bring to us, and we could offer him the broadness of experience through the things we're doing in our company."

They talked about it for a while and decided how they might best implement the director's suggestion. Then a few days later, the president called Jim into his office to ask him if he'd be interested in the suggestion made by the outside director.

Jim was absolutely delighted. He saw it as an opportunity to broaden his experience, which was exactly what he wanted to accomplish. The president saw it as an opportunity to accomplish not only Jim's personal objectives, but the objectives of the organization as well.

Unusual? Yes. Is it the kind of opportunity you can all take advantage of pretty often? No, certainly not. It is simply an example. It's a reminder to consider the objectives of the individuals in the organization when you're determining the objectives of the organization. If the individual's and the organization's objectives can be made to parallel each other, you stand a significantly improved chance of successfully implementing your plan.

32

Divergent Philosophies

A company's planning team is meeting to develop its strategic plan. Six or eight executives walk into a conference room to discuss where the company is, where it's going, and how it will get there. From their conversation, it appears that the team is splitting into two groups. About half the people in the room seem to be joining the "short-term" camp; the other half, the "long-term" camp.

The short-term people emphasize immediate profit. They might say something like, "The thing we really care about is profit. We want to get that bottom line. And we want to get it right now."

And those short-term folks might conclude that the way to get that near-term profit is to do the same things they've been doing, only better. They don't want to consider developing new products or finding new markets. They simply want to do a better job at the same old thing. They want to sell their current line of products and services to their current markets, to penetrate deeper into that marketplace, and to improve their current operations, thus increasing profit.

The people on the other side of the table—those in the long-term camp—might become frustrated with all this short-term thinking. Looking at the short-term folks, the longer-term thinkers might say, "Look, we agree with you. We agree that profit is important. But our time frame is different from yours." The long-term folks might continue, "We look for profit, not now, but further in the future. If you allow us some time, allow us to be creative either in developing products or services or in developing new markets, then we'll bring you more profit than you've ever dreamed of. You need simply allow us to grow."

And on and on goes this most common argument.

Clearly, I'm exaggerating when I describe a planning team splitting into two camps. No such physical division actually occurs. But there are two fundamental philosophies—short-term and long-term—which frequently surface at strategy sessions. You'll have to be prepared to deal with the potential resultant conflict.

If the folks in the long-term camp win the argument, there are two fundamental ways the company can grow. It can develop new products and services, or it can develop new markets. For either of these two paths to growth, the firm can choose to do something just a little bit different or something very different from what it is currently doing. It can, for example, choose to develop new products and services that are related to its current products and services (same technology, same manufacturing or delivery process). Or it can develop new products and services that are unrelated to the company's current products and services.

Similarly, it may enter new markets which are either related or unrelated to its current markets.

Generally, it takes more time to develop new products and services or new markets than to improve current operations. If the time required increases as we elect to develop products and services, what happens to the risk factor? Generally, it increases. Typically, it is more risky to expand outside of the present business, that is, outside present products and services and present markets. This is so because new products, services, and markets involve development in unfamiliar territory.

There are instances, however, when it is more risky

to take the short-term approach, to stay with current products and services. It is more risky to do so when there is significant change in the marketplace, either on the growth side or on the decline side of the product/service life cycle (see Figure 32-1). On the growth side, computer manufacturers, for example, would be very foolish to attempt selling, in the long term, current products and services to current markets. Technological advances in their industry make it impossible for them to think in terms of doing the same thing—same products, same markets—three years from today, for example, that they do today. That market and the technology on which it's based are simply changing too fast.

The change in the marketplace may also be on the decline side, that is, where the products and services are nearing the end of their life cycles. Here, too, it is risky to think in terms of selling the same products and services to the same markets. It is no longer appropriate

Figure 32-1. Product/service life cycle.

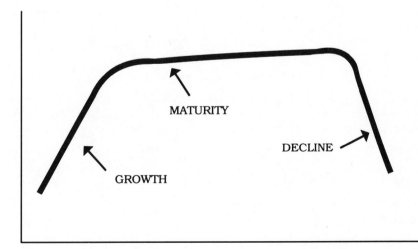

for Oldsmobile to hold on to a large V8 internal combustion engine for a super-powered convertible. That car doesn't exist any longer because of significant change in the marketplace which began with the first Arab oil embargo in 1973.

There isn't any one right way for a company to grow, no singular answer that says, "Develop products and services but not markets," no singular rule that states, "Don't dare move into unrelated markets." It depends on the firm's position in the marketplace—its internal strengths and weaknesses and its external opportunities and threats. Here, like everyplace else, there's no substitute for management judgment.

33

Break Before
Strategizing

After you've completed your situation analysis and developed your mission statement and your objectives, you should next take a break and give your planning team some rest time before beginning strategy-setting sessions. If you're using the typical three-consecutive-day planning retreat, try to finish setting objectives about the middle of the second afternoon. And don't return to your sessions until after breakfast the next morning.

You should take this break for a couple of reasons. The obvious reason is that planning is just plain difficult. Not only is it physically difficult to live in a conference room for three consecutive days, but it's emotionally and mentally tough as well.

It's so difficult, in fact, that on the second afternoon you may suffer from "second-day syndrome." Second-day syndrome is like going camping with two close friends—and being forced by continuous rain to remain together in a small tent for three straight days. Funny thing—your two friends are beginning to go crazy. While you, of course, are absolutely sane. Well, that's "second-day syndrome." About the same thing happens in the conference room. You get the feeling you've just got to get out.

Perhaps more significant, however, is the less obvious reason to break before strategizing. Between objective setting and strategizing, you're about to change the way you think. During your situation analysis and objective setting—the process steps you tackled on the first two days of your meeting—you were very analytical in your thought. You analyzed your internal strengths and weaknesses, your external opportunities and threats. You were careful to quantify your objectives.

Now you're going to turn your attention toward a nonanalytical way of thinking. You're going to strategize. You're going to invent, to create, to innovate. You're going to go from what psychologists call "left-brain thinking" to "right-brain thinking." And you don't make that transition simply by downing another cup of coffee, hurrying back to your chair, and attempting to discuss strategies.

You need to go away to do some reflective thinking, to ponder the issues you've earlier discussed. Then you'll be ready to return to the conference room, not just rested, but also prepared to think creatively.

It's also worth remembering that you don't invent things in committees. Innovation begins within the mind of a single individual. So the break before strategizing offers the opportunity for individuals to get their creative juices flowing and sleep on their thoughts. Then (you hope) they'll return to the conference room with more creative ideas the next morning, when the planning team can turn those creative ideas into strategies.

34

The SW-OT Matrix

Imagine that you're participating as a planning team member in developing your organization's strategic plan. In the first two days of its planning sessions, your team has developed its situation analysis (strengths, weaknesses, opportunities, and threats), its mission statement, and a number of quantified objectives. And now, on the third and final day of the planning sessions, you and your team have just walked into the conference room to develop your strategies. Look at the walls. They're covered with large sheets of paper, upon which are written statements—lots of them.

The sheets on one side of the room were completed during the situation analysis session. The first of those sheets reads, "These are our internal strengths." The next sheet lists internal weaknesses; the next, external opportunities; the next, external threats. On the far side of the room are your mission statement, a reminder list, and your objectives. Next you've got some assumptions, a pro forma income statement that will become an appendix to the plan—in all, seventeen sheets of paper containing thirty-six separate statements.

It's somewhat intimidating to walk into the conference room, look at all the statements you earlier devel-

---

Note: SW-OT Matrix is a registered trademark of William S. Birnbaum.

oped, and think, "All we have to do now is develop strategies." You simply must decide how you're going to go from here (your situation analysis) to there (your objectives).

The SW-OT Matrix

What you need is a tool you can use to pull one issue at a time down from the walls of the room. So you can deal with a single issue at a time, rather than trying to deal with thirty-six all at once.

A tool useful for this application is the *SW-OT Matrix*™. First, I'll apologize for never having thought of a pretty name for the SW-OT Matrix. But the name really tells the story. "SW-OT" stands for strengths, weaknesses, opportunities, and threats. And "matrix" suggests that you're going to arrange items in a square and look for interrelationships among them.

To develop the SW-OT Matrix, you list internal factors—strengths and weaknesses—in one dimension and external factors—opportunities and threats—in the other (see Figure 34-1). Then you look for particular relationships between those internal and external factors.

Defensive Strategies

Recall that you have a list of external threats hanging on the wall of your conference room. You might look at each of those threats on the list and ask, "When are we especially vulnerable to each of those threats?" The answer, of course, is that you're most vulnerable to a particular threat when you have one or more internal weaknesses which relate to that threat.

Start another sheet of paper and head it "Defensive Strategies" (see Figure 34-2). Then list your first external

Figure 34-1. The SW-OT™ matrix.

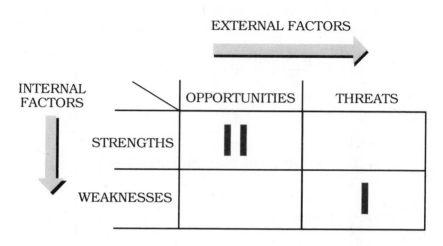

threat. Perhaps that first threat reads, "Our major competitor is going off-shore for low-cost production."

Having listed that threat, next consider which of your internal weaknesses align with that specific threat, thus making you especially vulnerable, and list them on that same piece of paper. For instance, internal weakness number one might read, "We have obsolete factory equipment, making our production costs high." That weakness seems to correspond to the particular external threat you're considering. Internal weakness number two might mention your poor balance sheet. It too relates, for that poor balance sheet would prohibit the capital investment required to reduce your manufacturing costs.

After having identified all the internal weaknesses that relate to the external threat under consideration, write the word "strategy." Then consider, "What are we going to do about this particular threat combined with its corresponding weaknesses? How will we deal with this situation? What is our strategy?" You won't forget the thirty-six statements on seventeen sheets of paper covering the walls. You'll use that information as back-

Figure 34-2. The defensive strategies sheet.

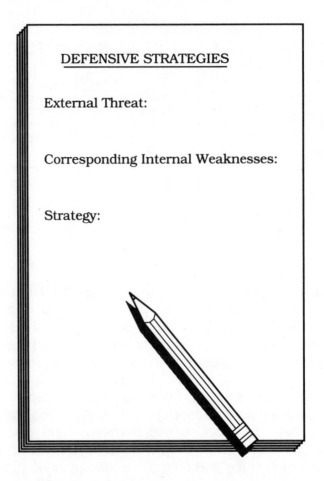

drop to your strategy discussions. But for now, focus your attention on the subject at hand—on that external threat you're considering, along with its corresponding internal weaknesses. Deal with one issue at a time.

Continue to evolve defensive strategies for each of your external threats, one at a time, until you've exhausted your list. If you earlier identified four external threats, you'll have four defensive strategic discussions, each leading to a defensive strategy or to a set of defensive strategies.

Strategies Built on Strength

Now you can turn your attention to the brighter side of the coin, recalling that earlier in the planning process you identified a number of external opportunities. But are those opportunities really for you? They are only if you possess the internal strengths that are both necessary and sufficient to go get those opportunities. Here, you're dealing with a relationship between external opportunities and internal strengths.

Start with a new sheet of paper and head it "Strategies Built on Strength" (see Figure 34-3). Next list the first of the opportunities from your opportunities list. Perhaps it reads, "Emerging market demand for a portable moisture monitor with an improved time constant."

Next, decide which of your internal strengths correspond to that external opportunity. Suppose one internal strength reads, "We have a sales force in place in the market area where that opportunity exists." Another strength reads, "We have additional capacity in R&D to develop the new product." You're aligning the particular opportunity with its corresponding internal strengths.

Before you develop strategies to go get the opportunity, you have to ask one very important question: "Are those corresponding internal strengths both necessary *and* sufficient to take advantage of the opportunity?" That is, do you have the necessary strengths to win if you do go after the opportunity?

If your answer to that most important question is "yes," next ask, "What is our strategy? How will we go get the opportunity?"

When you later apply that strategy to take advantage of that opportunity, it will, of course, take you toward

Figure 34-3.   The strategies-built-on-strength sheet.

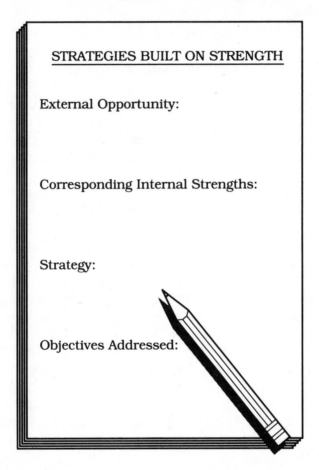

STRATEGIES BUILT ON STRENGTH

External Opportunity:

Corresponding Internal Strengths:

Strategy:

Objectives Addressed:

your objectives—because the objectives are your description of "where we wish to arrive, and when." So now,
you can add one more item to your paper and call it
"Objectives Addressed." After all, if that strategy is any
good at all, it's going to take you toward at least one of
your objectives. If not, forget the strategy.

Next consider your second external opportunity, list
its corresponding strengths, develop strategies, and cite

the objectives addressed. Then consider the third opportunity. Then the fourth. And continue developing strategies built on strength until you've exhausted your list of external opportunities.

Other Uses of the SW-OT Matrix

One question you might ask is, "What about the other two boxes in the SW-OT Matrix?" Might not an external threat align with some internal strengths, or an external opportunity with some internal weaknesses?

Clearly there are some issues which will not fall neatly into either of the two boxes we've discussed but will fall into one of the other two boxes. Or they may fall outside the model entirely.

First let's look at an example of an issue that fell into the threats-strengths category—the upper right corner of the SW-OT Matrix. The management team at one company was absolutely paranoid about the possibility that its workers would unionize. The number one threat that came up during its situation analysis was "Here comes the union." But if you were to look around the organization, you'd find absolutely nothing that made the company vulnerable to a union. Wages and salaries were in order. Working conditions were excellent. When an occasional grievance came up, two guys jumped on it, making it go away within half an hour. The company was absolutely not vulnerable to union organizing.

Nonetheless, you could not go into a planning retreat with this particular management team without the union threat emerging early in the discussion. If you were to place this issue on the SW-OT Matrix, you'd probably set it in the upper right—at the alignment of external threats and internal strengths.

On its defensive strategies sheet, the planning team listed "Threat #1: Here comes the union." Then it looked at its list of internal weaknesses, looking for a match between one or more of those weaknesses and the union threat. But no one could find a single corresponding weakness. So for "corresponding weaknesses" the facilitator wrote "none specific." But the planning team wanted to strategize about the union. And it did. It wrote four strategies to counter the union threat. Those four strategies had one thing in common—each of them began with the word "continue." Thus the four strategies actually reaffirmed the fact that the organization was doing things right regarding the union issue. And while the discussion landed in an unusual corner of the SW-OT Matrix, the process worked just fine.

For an example of the use of the opportunities-weakness box, the lower left-hand box of the model, consider one company that manufactured electronic power supplies—very high quality, very low volume. This company's power supplies were used in military, space, and high-end industrial applications. The production process included much hand labor, much inspection, little automation. Certainly the products weren't cheap. While compiling its opportunities list, the planning team listed the demand for very large quantity, very low price power supplies—real cheapies—for application in kitchen appliances.

When the planning team arrived at the "Strategies Built on Strength" portion of its discussions, the planning team wrote the opportunity on a fresh sheet of paper and asked, "Which of our internal strengths would support our going after this opportunity?" The managers looked at the wall where the internal strengths were listed—nothing. They had not a single internal strength to support going after that opportunity. The company was a high quality, low quantity operation. The opportunity called for high quantity, low price. Just the opposite. An entirely different business.

After a brief discussion about this "no-match" situation, the facilitator drew a diagonal line through the entire sheet of paper, in effect, crossing out that opportunity. Sure, it was an opportunity. But an opportunity for someone else. Not for this particular company.

That diagonal line had significant value for the organization. For three months prior to that meeting, the company's managers had been debating the merits of going after that "low-end" business. Here, top management developed a common vision regarding the opportunity's lack of fit and agreed to "killing" it.

Let's look at a case where the SW-OT Matrix might miss entirely, that is, the discussion might not land in any of the four quadrants. A few years back, one of our client companies was outgrowing its facility. At its then-current growth rate, it had to move in about five years. Five years! That's not a strength, a weakness, an opportunity, or a threat. But it is an issue. It's something management should talk about during strategic planning meetings.

Someone in the organization, after all, should pay attention to this requirement. If something isn't done about it soon, before they knew it, management would have only three years . . . then two. Then it would have a weakness. So it entered this issue as a note on its reminder list and, during strategy sessions, made sure to address it. Per the resultant strategy, the vice-president and the production manager became the "facilities planning committee." They committed to contact local real estate agents to search for larger facilities.

Reviewing the Results of the SW-OT Matrix

The SW-OT Matrix, just like any other model, is not perfect. It will generate about 90 percent of the discussions you'll need. Then you'll have to do some "clean-up." You'll have to look back at your lists and ask, "Did we really address each of our weaknesses?" If not, you may need to develop a strategy specifically to deal with a particular weakness or two. Also, did you address each of your objectives to your satisfaction? Sure, you listed each objective in the "Objectives Addressed" portion of your "Strategies Built on Strengths" sheets. But did you hit each hard enough? Can you really achieve that 13 percent operating profit? Or will the strategies as you've written them get you only 11.5 percent? If only 11.5 percent, you'd better develop another strategy specifically to boost operating profit. In either of these two cases—addressing a specific weakness or an objective—you might develop a category of strategies called "Other Strategies." And, by the way, you might not be able to develop a strategy to achieve 13 percent operating profit. If that's the case, you'll have to reduce the profit objective to 11.5 percent.

Speaking of addressing your objectives, we should discuss a "second school of thought." Many planners would prefer to develop strategies based on objectives, rather than on the alignment of threats with weaknesses and opportunities with strengths.

In fact, it might seem more logical to begin with objectives and from those objectives develop strategies by asking, "How in the world are we going to accomplish that objective?" For example, you might have set an objective to achieve 13 percent operating profit by the end of the third year. Couldn't you then go ahead and develop a strategy designed to achieve this objective directly and forget about strengths, weaknesses, opportunities, and threats—that is, forget about the SW-OT Matrix?

No, not really. You might say you're doing it, but in actual practice you need to think in terms of strengths, weaknesses, opportunities, and threats. Try this. Develop a strategy to boost operating profit from 11.5 percent to 13.0 percent. In developing your strategy, try not to think about your strengths, weaknesses, opportunities, or threats.

You can't do it, can you? Even if you don't draw the SW-OT Matrix on a piece of paper, you're building it in your mind.

35

Linking the Strategic Plan to Management by Objectives

Imagine you're on the planning team for an organization that employs its own direct sales force, and you've just written a strategy calling for training the sales force. After writing that strategy, you might look around the room and ask, "Who's going to do it?" For you know that writing a strategy is one thing; actually accomplishing it is something else again. And you can't hope to accomplish the strategy at all if you don't *reduce it to work.*

So you ask, "Who's going to do it?" Pretty soon a fellow raises his hand and volunteers that the strategy is in his area of responsibility. To no one's surprise, the volunteer is Marty Marketeer. Indeed, the strategy does fall into his area of responsibility—that of the sales and marketing department. So right there, at your strategy session, after writing the strategy on your large flipchart easel pad, you write the words, "Responsible manager: Marty Marketeer." And then you look at Marty and ask,

"Marty, when can we expect you to accomplish this strategy of training the sales force?"

Naturally, Marty pauses for a moment, thinks, and answers, "How about June 15?" "Fine," the planning team agrees. And the facilitator writes the words, "Due date: June 15."

By setting a due date for the strategy, you've established an objective for an individual—for Marty. You've linked the strategic planning process to management by objectives.

Certainly, there are those who have criticized the technique of management by objectives. They've said, "Management by objectives is fine, except that most of the time, most of the managers don't know what most of the objectives are." Well, Marty not only knows what his objective is, but his objective is "pushing" in the same direction as the objectives of the organization. So are all the other individuals' objectives which come from your strategic plan.

Let's take this process one step further. Since Marty is pretty smart, he writes his objective down on a piece of paper. So even before the plan is published, he has a record of his specific responsibilities. Then, after the strategy sessions, Marty goes back to his sales and marketing department, calls his key managers together, and says to them, "You wouldn't believe what I just committed us to do."

A couple of points here. First, Marty has taken responsibility for a *strategy* at the corporate (or division) level and that strategy has become an *objective* at the department level. The old saying is, "If you work for me, then my strategy is your objective."

A second point: Marty now has the opportunity to make use of the team planning process within his own department and to utilize that team approach in developing the necessary tactics (action steps) to implement the strategy—to train the sales force. More on this point in the chapter about action planning (Chapter 42).

36

Pre-Planning Forms

During 1980, when we began assisting client company managers in developing their strategic plans, we started each strategy session with a blank sheet of paper. Without benefit of any prepared notes, we'd facilitate the planning team's developing lists of internal strengths and weaknesses and external opportunities and threats. That "start-from-scratch" system left us with a number of significant problems.

First, the members of the planning team didn't get "warmed up" to the process. Sure, they all read the articles we distributed, but they hadn't been thinking about the subject of strategic planning in the context of their own organization. That made for a terribly slow start. And because the members of the planning team hadn't been stimulated to think strategically, the quality of the resultant plans may have suffered as well.

Another problem with beginning with a blank sheet of paper is that we wasted a whole bunch of time. Even on topics where we had overwhelming agreement, we still went through a lengthy discussion to discover that such agreement already existed. So we spent almost as much time on issues for which we already had agreement as on those for which we needed to develop such agreement.

Yet another problem with starting from scratch was

that the team frequently failed to discuss sensitive information. That is, managers feared bringing up important, though controversial, topics. So a number of critical issues simply failed to be addressed.

In 1981, we wised up. We decided to solve these problems by developing a set of *pre-planning forms.* We designed those forms in order to:

- Get all the folks on the planning team thinking strategically prior to our planning sessions.
- Save time in developing the strategic plan.
- Provide a relatively safe way to bring up controversial topics.

Over a period of a year or so, we developed a number of pre-planning forms. Let's look at those forms.

The Discussion Topics Form

We developed the Discussion Topics form to serve as an aid to the facilitator of the planning sessions. The form helps to uncover the topics which are on the minds of the members of the planning team. Thus, it's useful in developing an agenda for the strategy sessions.

This simple, one-page form challenges the respondents with three "fill-in-the-blank" responses, as follows:

1. At our upcoming strategy sessions, we'll probably discuss the following topics:

    a. _____

    b. _____

    c. _____

2. Some topics we probably won't discuss are:

a. _____

b. _____

c. _____

3. Some topics I'm particularly eager to discuss are:

a. _____

b. _____

c. _____

We ask each member of the planning team to complete this form and send it (or a copy of it) *anonymously* to us (or to whomever will facilitate the strategy sessions).

Upon receipt of all of the participants' forms, we compile the inputs. Those compiled lists provide us with a wealth of information useful in facilitating the strategy sessions.

For one, the answers to the first statement offer us a "feel" for the expectations of the planning team and thus provide a useful input in developing the agenda for the meeting.

In compiling the answers to the second statement, we learn of the topics which the planning team members feel they'll *not* deal with at the sessions. Interestingly, there are two reasons why an individual may feel the team will not deal with a particular topic at the strategy sessions. First, the topic may simply be too mundane, simply not worth the time of the planners—like the color of the stripes in the parking lot.

The second reason a planner may feel the team will not discuss a particular topic is that it's too controversial. It just isn't "safe." To know which one of those two reasons led the planner to judge the topic would not be discussed, we need simply look to the last statement, the "I'm eager to discuss . . ." one. If an individual lists a topic in response to the second statement ("probably won't discuss") and again in response to the third statement ("eager to discuss"), that issue is important to the individual. And it's our job as facilitators to see that the topic is addressed during the strategy sessions.

Because a number of highly sensitive comments appear on the Discussion Topics form, we don't share it with the planning team. Instead, we use it as our guide in facilitating the strategy sessions.

The Company Emphasis Form

The Company Emphasis form is, admittedly, something of an oversimplification, for in two short pages we suggest that there are five fundamental emphases (or philosophies, or cultures) which organizations may embrace:

1. Market emphasis
2. Products/services emphasis
3. Technology emphasis
4. Finance emphasis
5. Security emphasis

The form includes a short paragraph describing the characteristics and vulnerabilities of organizations having each emphasis. Here are some samples:

1. *Market Emphasis.* Companies that place their emphasis on the market feel that "the market is king." These organizations are led by individuals with strong marketing backgrounds. Their governing objectives will typically include sales growth rate and market share. These firms allocate considerable resources to market research, advertising, and promotion. The vulnerability of the market-emphasis organization may be product obsolescence, high costs, low quality, or poor liquidity.

2. *Product Emphasis.* Companies with a product emphasis follow the formula "A fine product sells itself." Such companies are managed by individuals with backgrounds in production and/or engineering. Product quality is of utmost importance. The organization dedicates resources to manufacturing, quality assurance, and purchasing. Its vulnerabilities lie in its potentially high costs and its failure to accurately identify market demands.

3. *Technology Emphasis.* Companies with technology emphasis feel "the market wants the latest technology." Almost without exception, they are led by engineers. They stress new products and dedicate their resources to research and development. Their vulnerability often lies in marketing; they fail to develop dominant (high market share) products and are outsold by their competitors.

4. *Finance Emphasis.* Organizations emphasizing finance believe, more than anything else, that "the bottom line counts." Such companies are, generally, led by managers having backgrounds in finance. They stress management by financial ratios—in particular, return on invested capital. Their resources go toward establishing and maintaining tight financial controls. Their vulnerabilities lie in marketing; they often enter unknown markets, suffer product obsolescence, and lack a clear company image.

5. *Security Emphasis.*Companies which emphasize security stress "balance and control." Such firms are managed by administrators who stress continuity and survival. Interestingly, these organizations place far more importance on their balance sheet than on their income statement. They invest resources in an ongoing attempt to acquire assets and reduce debt. Also, they are characterized by top-heavy staff. They are vulnerable from just about every direction.

Following those descriptive paragraphs, we present a number of "food-for-thought" questions, such as:

- Can you think of two or three organizations that fit each of the above categories?
- Do you think that a specific company emphasis is appropriate to particular products or industries?
- Might a firm's emphasis change as it grows and matures?
- Do you feel that an organization's emphasis changes as its products or services mature?

We ask each member of the planning team to spend thirty minutes or so with this form reading the descriptions of each of the five company emphases and then considering each of the food-for-thought questions. If they prefer, team members can discuss their answers with other members of the planning team or anyone else they'd like to. But they don't have to discuss them at all. They simply have to give the matter some thought.

We consider this form a "warm-up," an aid in getting ready to think strategically, as each of the planning team members will have to do during the upcoming strategy sessions.

The Strengths, Weaknesses, Opportunities, Threats Form

The Strengths, Weaknesses, Opportunities, Threats form saves time during our strategy sessions because it means we don't have to begin with a blank sheet of paper in developing our situation analysis. The form contains the four elements of the situation analysis: Internal Strengths, Internal Weaknesses, External Opportunities, and External Threats.

1. I believe our most significant internal strengths are:

   a. _____

   b. _____

   c. _____

2. Our most significant internal weaknesses are:

    a. _____

    b. _____

    c. _____

3. Our most significant external opportunities are:

    a. _____

    b. _____

    c. _____

4. Our most significant external threats are:

    a. _____

    b. _____

    c. _____

Each member of the planning team fills out the form and sends it (or a copy of it) *anonymously* to us (or to whomever will facilitate the planning sessions). Then we compile the answers we receive from each member of the planning team and share the input at the opening of the first strategy session. Thus we have a head start in developing consensus on our situation analysis.

37

The Written Plan

Here's a "suggested" table of contents for a strategic plan—"suggested" because there's no right or wrong way for the strategic plan to appear. Rather, it should be organized as required for a particular firm.

We've found over the years, however, that an outline that pretty much follows this suggested table of contents provides a pretty good starting point for most organizations.

TABLE OF CONTENTS

The first thing to note is that the order in which the various elements appear in the plan differs from the order in which we developed them. In developing the plan, you began by identifying your key success factors and then itemizing your internal strengths and weaknesses and your external opportunities and threats. Then you developed your mission statement and objectives and finally, your strategies.

But in the written plan, we suggest a somewhat different order. That's because, while the process of developing the plan followed a logical order (addressing planning's three key questions of "Where are we today?" "Where do we wish to arrive, and when?" and "How do we get from here to there?" the written plan is constructed for the convenience of the *reader*, whose needs are different. This is true even if the reader happens to be one of the developers of the plan who returns to the written document three months later.

The next thing we'll note about the plan is its brevity—twenty-five to thirty pages or so, often less. If you can't say it briefly, you probably don't have anything to say. Keep it short.

The Introduction

The plan should begin with an introduction, an opportunity for the CEO (or the "boss person" by whatever title) to discuss the "why?" of the strategic plan: what benefits the company hopes to obtain through developing the plan. There also may be a word or two about the history of the organization, its values, and its culture. In short, the introduction is the boss person's opportunity to discuss the philosophies of the organization and what the management team hopes to accomplish in developing the plan. It should probably take up a page or so.

The Mission Statement

Nothing is more fundamental to the enterprise than its relationship to its customer. It's the mission statement that describes that most important relationship. Thus, the mission statement should appear very early in the written plan.

Briefly, the mission statement identifies the business the company is in, identifies the company's market, and describes its position in its industry. That is, it describes how the company's products or services are differentiated from those of its competition. The mission statement offers the reader a sense of the management team's shared vision and lays the foundation for all other elements of the plan.

Key Success Factors

Next are the key success factors, the two or three specific ingredients required to "win" within the industry—those factors you *must* be good at in order to succeed. In fact, if you were good at those few activities only, you could afford to be mediocre at everything else and still be successful.

Because the key success factors are so crucial, they appear pretty early in the plan.

Assumptions

Since the future is unknown, you've had to make a number of assumptions in developing your plan—assumptions about the economy, your customer's future desires, your competitors. Those assumptions appear in your plan just before your objectives because they relate to those objectives: While the external world continues to be pretty much as you've assumed it will be, you view your objectives as being attainable. But those assumptions had better hold true. And that means you'll have to monitor those assumptions along with your objectives.

Objectives

Next, of course, are your objectives—the quantified expression of "where we wish to arrive, and when." Hopefully, you've kept your objective list short, limiting it to around six or seven objectives.

You should also have prioritized your objectives, either numerically (1, 2, 3, etc.) or, if you're unable to decide if objective 3 is really more important than objective 4, by identifying three levels—"A," "B," and "C."

Situation Analysis

While developing the plan, you answered the question, "Where are we today?" And the answer to that question came in the form of four lists: "Internal Strengths," "Internal Weaknesses," "External Opportunities," and "External Threats." Here's where they belong in the written plan.

Strategies

Strategies come next. First you present the strategies just as you developed them—as defensive strategies and as strategies built on strength. Defensive strategies are those developed to counter internal weaknesses that render the organization vulnerable to external threats. Strategies built on strength are those which utilize internal strengths to take advantage of external opportunities.

Since the world isn't neat enough for all strategies to fit nicely into these two categories, you have a third category—"Other Strategies."

Summary of Strategies

When you formulated your strategies, you related internal weaknesses to external threats in developing defensive strategies. Then you related internal strengths to external opportunities in developing strategies built on strength. While this process works very well for *developing* your strategies, its written format is difficult to follow on paper. Because the strategies appear in no particular order, they're tough to review.

Naturally, you want to do everything you can to make reviewing the plan a "friendly" experience. So you need a written format which presents your strategies in some more logical order. Thus the summary of strategies.

There's nothing magic about the categories within that summary—you simply make them appropriate to your specific strategies. Typical titles, though, are marketing, product (or service) development, and organizational and human resource strategies.

Appendices

The final element in your written plan are the appendices, the catch-all for whatever else you'd like to attach to the plan. Appendices may include a customer profile, a resource allocation spreadsheet, or a list of development projects. A common part of the appendix section is the pro forma (projected) income statement.

Remember, this is a suggested format for the written plan. Sure, it works. But what you really want is one that best serves your organization. You can start with this one. But be watchful for opportunities to change the format to benefit your organization.

38

The Rise and Fall of Portfolio Analysis

Thus far in Part II, we've been discussing the *process* of strategy development. Now we'll spend some time on *content* of strategy. Specifically, we'll examine a couple of business models, one in this chapter and one in the next.

I'll begin with a confession. I love business models. I love them because they offer us a framework in which to think deeply about our business. But, at the same time, I don't really trust business models, because they can be misleading. Consider, for example, the *portfolio analysis model.*

Among many well-known business models, the portfolio analysis model remains the most interesting for three reasons. First, the model has, over the years, been the most popular of all business models. It was popularized by the Boston Consulting Group and adapted for use by many U.S. corporations. Second, the portfolio analysis model is elegant and poses a very inviting argument, so inviting, in fact, that it's been used in ap-

Note: This discussion of the *portfolio analysis model* is based on "The Experience Curve-Reviewed, IV. The Growth Share Matrix or The Product Portfolio," *Perspectives*, No. 135. Reprinted by permission from The Boston Consulting Group, Inc., Boston, Massachusetts. © 1973.

plications where it doesn't fit. And that brings us to our third and final source of interest. During recent years, the model has come under fire and has been criticized as faulty because of its too-frequent misapplication.

In the following discussion, we'll analyze the portfolio analysis model and see how to benefit from it *even in applications where it doesn't fit.*

Like so many business models, the portfolio analysis model is represented by a square. This particular square has two axes, one labeled "Market Growth Rate (Real)" and the other, "Relative Market Share" (see Figure 38-1).

Market Growth Rate

Market growth rate is the rate at which the total market (demand) for the product or service is increasing from one year to the next *in real terms,* independent of inflation. This growth rate is the *slope* of the product (or service) life cycle (see Figure 38-2). If market demand is increasing very fast—that is, the industry is enjoying rapid growth (the product or service is in its growth phase in Figure 38-2)—then that market appears toward the top of the portfolio analysis model (Figure 38-1). If, on the other hand, market demand for the product or service has flattened out (the product or service is in its maturity phase in Figure 38-2), then that market appears toward the bottom of the model (Figure 38-1).

Note the "10 percent real growth" line in Figure 38-2, which horizontally bisects the model. It is generally agreed that the 10 percent growth rate corresponds to the transition of the product or service from growth to maturity. That transition corresponds to the *shakeout* in the industry.

Relative Market Share

To understand the horizontal axis—*relative market share*—first we should talk about plain old *market share.*

Figure 38-1. Portfolio analysis model.

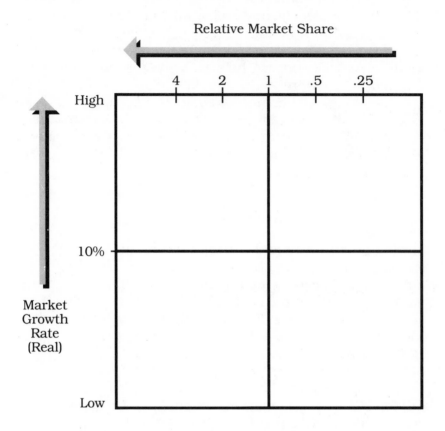

Market share is your level of annual sales divided by the annual sales of your entire industry for similar products or services.

Relative market share, a somewhat tougher concept, is your sales divided by *the sales of your major competitor*—again, for similar products or services.

Relative market share may seem like a strange concept. If you're the market leader, enjoying the largest market share in your industry, then your sales figure is larger than that of your largest competitor, the second

Figure 38-2. Product/service life cycle.

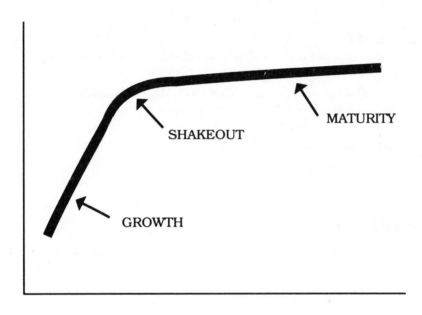

largest supplier. And your relative market share—your sales divided by the sales of your largest competitor—will therefore be greater than one. And since there's a vertical line labeled "1.0" right down the middle of the model, you as market leader will be represented by a point (though more typically a circle) on the left side of the model. But all of your competitors will be on the right side, because when calculating their own relative market shares, they will all divide their own sales by your sales, a larger number in every case.

That means that in any market, the leader will be *alone* on the left side of the model; *everyone* else will be on the right side. If, for example, the industry leader enjoys twice the sales of the nearest competitor, the leader can be represented by a circle in the left half of the diagram (see Figure 38-3). Note that the leader's circle is vertically below the number 2.0, indicating that that company enjoys a relative market share of 2.0 (because sales are twice that of the largest competitor). Also note that the competitor enjoying the second largest relative market share is represented by a circle under the number 0.5. That figures, since 0.5 is the inverse of 2.0.

Note that all of the other competitors are represented by circles farther and farther to the right as their relative market shares decrease. Note too that all of the competitors are represented by circles along a horizontal line. The location of that horizontal line is dependent upon the real market growth rate for the industry. The greater

Figure 38-3. Relative market share.

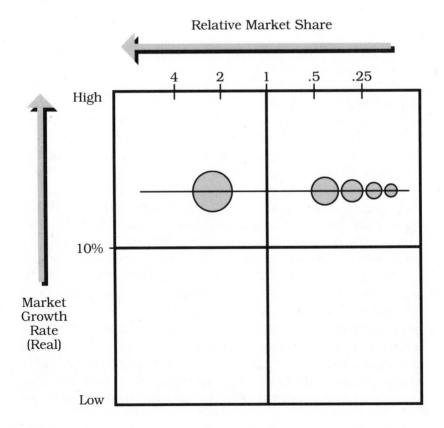

the growth rate, the higher the line on the model. And the more mature the industry, the lower the line.

The size of each circle is typically representative of relative market share. That's why the circles diminish in size from left to right.

Certainly, this seems an interesting academic exercise, and visually, it provides a feel for what's happening in the marketplace. But you can appreciate the real importance of the portfolio analysis model only after considering the significance of each of the model's four quadrants.

Rising Stars

Products (or services) located in the upper left quadrant of the model are called "rising stars," and they exist in an exciting world indeed. First, they're exciting because of rapid *growth,* with demand rising as a generous supply of new customers enter the marketplace. Sales figures increase industrywide.

The second reason our rising stars are exciting is that they're the market leaders—the "big kids on the block."

That's important, says The Boston Consulting Group, because of something they call the "experience curve" (see Figure 38-4). According to that curve, cumulative experience (market share over time) drives costs lower. As the leader in an industry enjoys a greater experience, thanks to greater market share over time, costs of production, marketing, and distribution all decline. Smaller producers—those having lesser experience (market share over time)—suffer higher costs. Note that competitor A, having more experience, enjoys costs lower than competitor B. Given the same market selling price, competitor A enjoys a greater profit (P_a) than does competitor B (P_b).

So having products or services in the upper left portion on the model—having "rising stars"—is clearly

Figure 38-4. The experience curve.

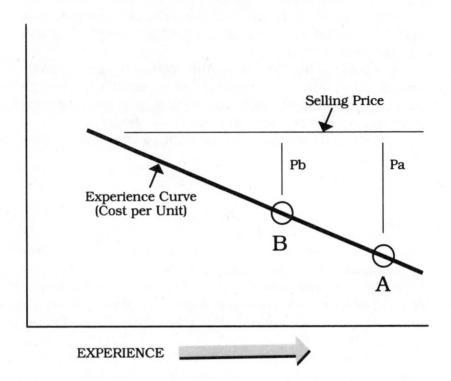

beneficial. Specifically, it's profitable. However, rising stars don't generate cash and increase bank balances. Because it takes cash to fuel their way up the growth curve, any cash they may generate is immediately rein-vested in growth—in increased inventory and accounts receivable, expanded production facilities, and (believe it or not) increased overhead.

Cash Cows

As exciting as rising stars are, they don't last forever. Optimistic sales forecasts to the contrary, the market will some day mature. Sooner or later, consumers will decide they need about as much of the product or service as they're currently buying, not 20 percent more. This corresponds to moving through and surviving the shakeout period (Figure 38-2). Following that shakeout, even the best rising star will fall to the lower left quadrant. There it becomes a "cash cow" (Figure 38-5).

Products become cash cows when just one thing— one very significant thing—changes. Since the product no longer enjoys rapid growth, cash is no longer needed

Figure 38-5. The four categories in portfolio analysis.

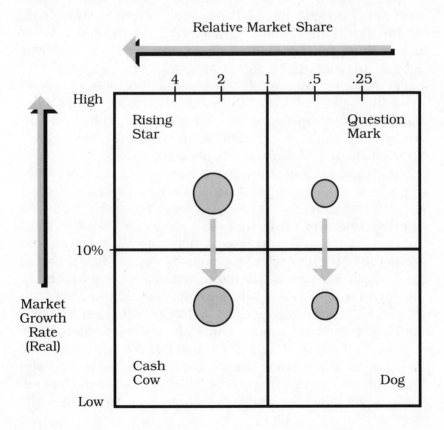

to support such growth. Sure, the greater relative market share still generates higher profits. In fact, since the shakeout is behind you and some of the weaker competitors are gone, profits may well be higher than ever. But cash is not required for growth. And that means the product or service generates cash—thus the name "cash cow."

Question Marks

Up to now, we've been talking about products and services enjoying leadership positions in their markets. We've concentrated on the left side of the model only.

But most products and services spend most of their lives on the right side of the model, *not* in market leadership positions. So it's important to understand what life is like on the right side of the portfolio analysis model. In the upper right quadrant are products and services called by one of two names, "problem child" or "question mark." I like the name "question mark" because it's descriptive of the situation; it implies an unknown. As you'll see in a moment, that unknown relates to a strategic decision you'll need to make.

Certainly, "question mark" products and services represent exciting situations. They're participating in a growth industry. But they're not making much profit. As the "smaller kid on the block," having a lesser relative market share and correspondingly higher relative cost (remember the experience curve in Figure 38-4), profits are lower. So you must make a decision—whether or not to invest in the product or service. If you invest in it, you're attempting to drive it to the left, that is, committing resources to capture more (relative) market share.

And if you succeed, that's great! You land on the left side of the model, you've got a rising star, and you take the lead in your marketplace. With increased market share over time, your profits increase. And when the market matures (it will), you will get yourself a "cash cow" with all its associated riches.

Dogs

If you don't succeed in driving your "question mark" to the left—if you don't take leadership in the market—then when the market matures, your product or service will fall to the lower right quadrant and you'll have a "dog" (Figure 38-5). It's in this "dog" category that most smaller businesses spend most or all of their lives—as marginal producers eking out a marginal profit in a no-growth marketplace.

In this no-growth dog category, few new customers enter the market—few new suppliers, too. The market is mature. All in all, it's pretty unexciting. With low relative market share, those suppliers in the dog category have relatively low profits. And they're stuck, because investing to capture market share is hardly a viable opportunity. Unlike growth markets, where you can gain market share by selling to some of the *new* customers entering the market, growth in mature markets means *taking customers away from somebody else.* That's always tough. And when you're a smaller supplier, taking sales away from a larger competitor is *very* tough—often impossible.

The Boston Consulting Group defines something called the "Success Triangle" (Figure 38-6). According to the success triangle, companies generate funds from "cash cows" in the lower left quadrant and invest those funds in "question marks" in the upper right quadrant. Naturally, they make that investment to increase market share. They hope to convert the "question marks" into "rising stars" (upper left quadrant). Then, over time as the market matures, those rising stars will become the cash cows of the future (lower left quadrant).

It's a grand plan. But it isn't for everyone. Because

Figure 38-6. The success triangle.

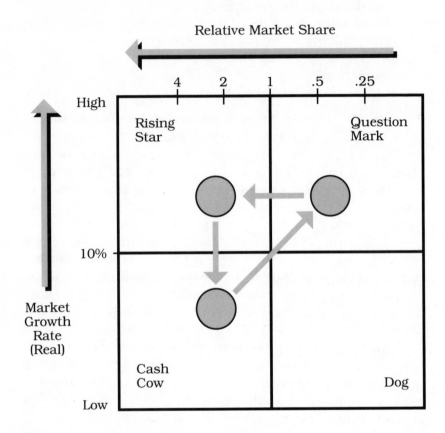

it necessitates becoming the dominant supplier in an industry. And few companies have the resources to "push" to the left, converting question marks to rising stars.

Misuses of the Model

It isn't surprising that most of the clients of The Boston Consulting Group are first, or at worst second, in their respective industries. After all, the model (along with The Boston Consulting Group) delivers a message to "dominate or divest"—that is, achieve a leadership position or get out. And this message is attractive only to the larger-share supplier.

But perhaps the model is wrong—or at least misleading. Perhaps there are situations where it doesn't work very well.

Let's pose an example. What would you suppose is the growth rate (in real terms) of the international automobile market? A pretty small number, maybe 2 or 3 percent; maybe as high as 5 percent. Certainly not more than 7 percent or so. Clearly, the worldwide automobile market is mature, growing at something less than 10 percent per year.

Now let's pick a company within that industry. What would you guess is the relative market share of Rolls-Royce Limited? Pretty low, right? So the conclusion is obvious: Rolls-Royce has a "dog" product.

But that conclusion is wrong! Rolls-Royce does *not* have a dog product. So the model doesn't work.

Or maybe we *misused* the model by incorrectly defining Rolls-Royce's market. We assumed that Rolls-Royce participates in the worldwide automobile market. But it doesn't. It doesn't even make an automobile. Not in the same sense that General Motors or Toyota make automobiles. Rolls-Royce makes something else—perhaps a penthouse suite on four wheels complete with bar and television set. However we describe its product, Rolls-Royce doesn't participate in the worldwide automobile market. Instead, Rolls-Royce sells a highly differentiated product to a narrow niche market.

Similarly, smaller market share suppliers can offer a product or service different from their competitors. Or they may focus on specific market niches. By redefining their market, small suppliers on the right of the model can "leap" to the left. Within their own *narrowly defined* niche markets, they can develop more profitable "rising stars" and "cash cows."

So while the Boston Consulting Group preaches "dominate or divest," we prefer to add one alternative strategy—*differentiate*. And it isn't necessary to differentiate by supplying a high-end "Rolls-Royce" product or service. Other bases for differentiation will do just as well—computer manufacturers who offer technology leadership, department stores that offer superior service, or software developers who address the unique requirements of a specific industry, for example.

Here's the point. Successfully differentiated products and services have one thing in common: They appeal to consumers who demand *attributes other than price.* That's important. Read it again: *attributes other than price.*

If buyers feel that other product attributes are more important than price, you've got the makings of a good differentiation strategy. And the portfolio analysis model, based entirely on the experience curve's cost (thus, price) relationship to market share, becomes invalid.

In short, the model works very well with commodity products where each one is just like the next. But it works hardly at all with well-differentiated products and services.

As our economy becomes increasingly dependent on services and information products, we're seeing more and more differentiation within narrower and narrower niche markets. In effect, we're going out of the business of supplying commodity products. So the portfolio analysis model continues to diminish in importance.

But discussing the model remains as valuable as ever. Even though you might conclude that the model doesn't fit your particular situation, it still provides enormous "food for thought." It forces you to think strategically about your business. And that's the most significant benefit you could hope to obtain from any business model.

39

Planning for Profit on Smaller Orders

In this chapter, we'll look at one more business model, not a marketing model but rather a financial model—a very useful, though rather unconventional, financial model.

Most companies set a minimum acceptable order level. Managers know intuitively that below some dollar amount an order is simply not profitable. But, too often, managers set their minimum order level too low, thus depressing profit.

This happens for a couple of reasons. First, managers dislike turning away orders, even small orders. Second, and more significantly, they lack techniques for analyzing profit for individual orders. Thus, they remain unaware of the extent to which smaller orders erode profit.

Unfortunately, conventional accounting techniques, while essential for reporting, provide poor tools for analyzing profit by order size. Using conventional techniques, managers allocate expenses either by *direct-labor hours* or by *dollar sales*. They should, instead, allocate a portion of expenses *by order*. That is, *they should allocate certain expenses equally against each order regardless of order size.*

Let's consider a simple example—a company manufacturing electronics equipment on a "per-order" basis. It costs about as much to set up production for a fifty-piece order as for a one-hundred-piece order of the same product. That setup cost is a per-order expense that remains substantially the same regardless of order size. Other per-order expenses include pulling parts from stock, issuing assembly instructions, and setting up production equipment.

Look at the Manufacturing Company's Income Statement (Figure 39-1). Suppose, during the year, the firm sells $1 million worth of equipment. Also, suppose that cost-of-goods-sold (cost of parts and materials, direct labor, and factory overhead) totals $600,000, 60 percent of sales. That leaves a gross profit of $400,000, 40 percent of sales.

To determine net profit, subtract expenses from gross profit. Expenses are funds spent, not on producing products, but on designing, marketing, and selling products and managing the business. These expenses include sales expense ($50,000), sales commissions expense ($50,000), production engineering expense ($30,000), research and development expense ($20,000), and general and administrative expense ($150,000). Total expenses are $300,000, 30 percent of sales. Subtracting total expenses from gross profit leaves a net profit of $100,000, 10 percent of sales.

This conventional income statement, like any other tool, has its limitations. It reports, not individually but *cumulatively*, all orders for the year. If you tried to use it to predict profit for individual orders, you'd find it seriously misleading. You'd erroneously conclude that *any order, regardless of size,* had associated expenses of 30 percent of sales. Also you'd conclude that each order offered a net profit of 10 percent of sales.

Clearly, this is wrong. You cannot use this conventional income statement to predict profit for individual orders. It is useless for that purpose because it fails to recognize per-order expenses and fails to allocate those expenses *by order.*

Figure 39-1. The manufacturing company's year-end income statement.

		Percent of Sales
Sales	$1,000,000	100%
Cost of goods sold	600,000	60
Gross profit	$ 400,000	40%

Expenses			
Sales	$ 50,000		
Sales commissions	50,000		
Production engineering	30,000		
R&D	20,000		
General and Administrative	150,000		
Total expenses		$300,000	30%
Net profit		$100,000	10%

To properly allocate per-order expenses, you'll need to know the total number of orders. Suppose that number is 200. Two hundred separate orders are required to sell $1 million worth of equipment—an average of $5,000 per order.

Next, you'll need to identify those expenses to allocate by order. Which specific expenses are of a per-order nature? Clearly, sales expense is one. Sales expense remains about the same regardless of order size. The sales staff spends about as much time in selling a $1,000, a $2,000, or a $3,000 order. Thus, you'll allocate the $50,000 sales expense over two hundred orders to obtain $250 per order (Figure 39-2).

Also, you should allocate production engineering expense by order. This expense is associated with preparing documentation for releasing orders to production. As documentation requirements are independent of order size, this expense is of a per-order nature. That's $30,000 divided by 200 orders, or $150 per order.

Clearly, some expenses are correctly allocated by the conventional method, by dollar sales. One such expense is sales commission expense. Obviously, the higher the dollar sale, the higher the sales commission. Thus, we allocate sales commissions of $50,000 over $1 million sales—that's 5 percent of sales.

Another expense correctly allocated by dollar sales is research and development. This expense does not relate to individual orders. Rather, it is justified by, and thus more closely relates to, sales volume. Allocating this expense by dollar sales, we find that $20,000 divided by $1 million sales equals 2 percent of sales.

Finally, we should allocate certain expenses partly by order and partly by dollar sales. General and administrative expense is of this type. Since the company manufactures its products on a per-order basis, it must purchase some parts and materials on a per-order basis. Those G&A expenses associated with per-order purchases should logically be allocated by order. Those G&A expenses associated with activities independent of individual orders should be allocated by dollar sales.

Let's assume the company has $20,000 in G&A expenses to be allocated by order and $130,000 in G&A expenses to be allocated by dollar sales. Then G&A expense allocated by order is $20,000 divided by two hundred orders, or $100 per order. G&A expense allocated by dollar sales is $130,000 over $1 million, or 13 percent of sales.

We've now uncovered the relationship between profit and order size (Figures 39-2 and 39-3). Obviously, profit

Figure 39-2. The manufacturing company's allocation of costs.

	Allocated By:	Average Order Size →			
Size of order (dollars)		$2,000	$5,000	$10,000	$20,000
Cost of goods sold		1,200	3,000	6,000	12,000
Gross profit		$ 800	$2,000	$ 4,000	$ 8,000
Expenses					
Sales expenses ($50,000)	200 orders	250	250	250	250
Production engineering expense ($30,000)	200 orders	150	150	150	150
Sales commissions ($50,000)	$1MM Sales	100	250	500	1,000
R&D expense ($20,000)	$1MM Sales	40	100	200	400
General/administrative ($20,000)	200 orders	100	100	100	100
General/administrative ($130,000)	$1MM Sales	260	650	1,300	2,600
Total expenses		900	1,500	2,500	4,500
Net profit (dollars)		($100)	$500	$1,500	$3,500
Net profit (as percent of sales)		(5%)	10%	15%	17.5%

increases as order size increases. More surprising, however, below the average-size order, profit falls dramatically. In fact, a $2,000 order actually produces a 5 percent loss!

Having discovered that the company is losing money on its smaller orders, management can adopt any one of several strategies. One obvious possibility is to simply increase the acceptable minimum order level. Another is to establish a finished goods inventory on more popular models. This would make production runs larger in size

Figure 39-3. The manufacturing company's profit by order size.

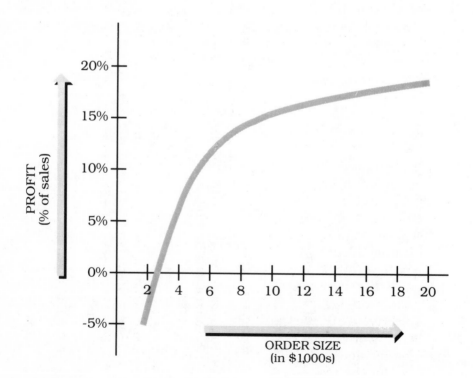

and, more significantly, fewer in number. This reduced number of production runs would, in turn, reduce both purchasing and production startup expenses. Sales expense would, of course, remain unaffected.

Another strategy is to adjust sales price by size of order. This, in effect, establishes a "setup" or "handling" charge in recognition of the per-order nature of certain expenses. For instance, a $300 setup charge on a $2,000 order would convert a $100 net loss to a $200 net profit (Figure 39-2).

To some degree, per-order expenses are present in every business. For example, it requires about as much time—and thus money—to acknowledge a $1,000 order as a $2,000 order, to prepare the shipping papers, to type the invoice, to solve a customer's problem, and to collect from a slow-paying account.

To determine profit by order size, identify per-order expenses and allocate those expenses by order. Knowing your profit by order size will enable you to make informed strategic decisions and, as a result, improve overall profit.

A contract manufacturing company analyzed its profit by size of order and discovered that among its twenty-seven accounts, the company was making a profit on the largest dozen accounts only. The smallest fifteen were running at break-even or loss. In effect, the largest twelve accounts were subsidizing all of the others.

During its strategic planning meetings, the company's management team decided to set an objective which would guide the company toward elimination of this problem. First, it considered setting an objective which would call for a minimum percentage business from the top ten accounts. Specifically, it discussed calling for obtaining 90 percent of revenue from these top ten.

At first glance, it seemed as if that objective would point the company in the right direction—toward emphasis on larger, more profitable accounts. Setting the objective at 90 percent of revenue, rather than 100 percent, would leave the door open for that occasional, smaller account with exceptional growth potential.

But the managers remembered another problem. Two

years earlier, the company had lost its top two accounts, both in the same year—certainly a major setback. With that loss fresh in the minds of management, the last thing in the world the company wanted to do was write an objective that would increase its vulnerability to its largest accounts. If anything, it wanted to decrease vulnerability to the loss of a very large account.

So the management team developed the concept of "mid-core accounts." It set an objective calling for obtaining 50 percent of sales revenue from accounts ranking 3 through 8. Naturally, the company doesn't pursue its objective by turning away additional business from its two largest accounts. Instead, it builds its mid-core accounts to balance any increase in business from the two largest accounts. And management is very selective about accepting business from smaller, less profitable accounts.

But note this. The objective still leaves the door open for those smaller accounts to show future potential for growth. The objective still leaves room for—indeed, calls for—managerial judgment, a necessary ingredient in working with any business model.

40

Successful Implementation Is No Accident

The 1970s saw progress in the development of tools and techniques for developing strategy. Unfortunately, the 1980s saw disappointment in the *implementation* of strategies developed using even the most up-to-the-minute techniques. Managers came to realize that it was one thing to develop a strategic plan and quite another to implement it successfully. So the focus has clearly turned toward implementation.

And implementation is tough, because it requires a combination of both "science" and "art." Implementation is science in that it deals with specific process steps, like developing detailed action plans, allocating resources, and conducting periodic follow-up meetings. Implementation is art in that it also deals with the "softer" side of management—the human resource issues, employee participation, communication, and commitment.

Most often, managers ask the question of "how to implement" far too late. They start thinking about implementation only after they've develop their strategies. That's a mistake. They should take implementation steps both before and during strategy development as well.

Imagine that we're walking up a hill, not just for the fun of it and not for the exercise but because we're going to develop our strategic plan while standing on top of the hill. Then, after we're finished developing our plan, we'll walk down the other side of the hill.

Walking up the hill corresponds to our getting ready to develop our plan. Standing on top of the hill corresponds to the time we're actually developing our plan. And walking down the hill corresponds to the time following our development of the plan.

There are specific implementation steps we should consider during each of these times: walking up, standing on top, and walking down. Let's look at each of these three sets of implementation steps separately.

Pre-Planning Implementation Steps

Well before our strategy sessions, we have opportunities to lay the groundwork for the successful implementation of our resultant strategies. The first step—perhaps the most important step—is to demonstrate managerial commitment to the planning process and to the resultant strategies within the plan. Management must demonstrate its commitment not just by word but by deed as well—by giving its own time to the planning process and by demonstrating readiness to allocate the necessary resources to the resultant strategies.

Next, the company must select the right planning team members. They'll come from the ranks of top management—the key functional managers. This brings to the strategy sessions the expertise necessary to develop the plan and makes possible the necessary immediate strategic decisions. More important yet, it involves the key executives in development of the plan, thus encouraging their commitment to the implementation they'll later direct.

Strategic planners must gather the right information

before developing their strategies. Not just the obvious—the financial reporting information—but also information about their customers and the benefits they seek in purchasing products and services. Planners must know why customers buy, and why they don't. They need information about the competition—their strengths, their weaknesses, and how their offerings compare. Successful strategies follow from the management team's full appreciation of the enterprise and its relationship to its marketplace. The team needs the right information to establish and update that teamwide awareness.

Also before planning, management should solicit input from company employees, to get them involved in the planning process and to flush out issues they feel are important. So they too *care* about the implementation of the resultant strategies.

This participation builds necessary commitment. Employees who have the opportunity to participate in their company's strategic plan feel a part of that plan. They're committed to the success of the plan and the successful implementation of the strategies within the plan.

At his company's strategic planning retreat, the vice-president of marketing for one of our client companies remarked, "The managers in our marketing department are anxious to see this plan. They've provided much of the initial input for this session, so they're looking forward to implementing the resultant strategies."

While-Planning Implementation Steps

During your strategic planning sessions, you have additional opportunities to encourage successful implementation of your resultant strategies. First, you can encourage participation from all members of your planning team. You can work toward rich, lively discussions on all issues, solicit input from the more hesitant, and, if necessary, temper the more domineering individuals. To do so, you must be sure the facilitator of your sessions has not only expertise in the planning process but also skill in handling the planning team's interpersonal dynamics.

You can also encourage implementation through focusing on your key success factors—on those few activities that will make you successful. Focusing on doing these "right things right" will concentrate resources on those factors which are most important.

You can encourage implementation by developing objectives measurable by your current reporting system. You'll be busy enough implementing your plan; don't pioneer a new reporting system if it isn't really necessary.

Also while planning, you can encourage successful implementation of your strategies through developing a balanced list of objectives and by having one or more objectives dealing with human resource issues, such as working conditions, career development, or benefit programs. Because more of your employees care about human resources than about sales volume and profit. Having a human resource objective, you'll have an answer when those employees—whose help you'll need in implementing your strategies—ask, "What's in it for me?"

You should also develop strategies built on your company's strengths. If you're strong in marketing, you'll best implement a strategy calling for promoting your way to success. If you're good at product development, you'd best *invent* your way to growth. And you shouldn't select a strategy just because it's popular, or because it worked for another company. It's got to work for you. It must be built on your own company's strengths.

Also, you'll have to consider available resources. That means you need to estimate the resources required to implement each strategy. You must be careful about overcommitting those resources, particularly people. There's a fine line between challenge, which encourages implementation, and overcommitment, which discourages implementation.

Finally, while developing your strategies, you should include a built-in monitoring system. Have a key executive volunteer to take on responsibility for implementing each strategy. That executive's name, along with a due date for completion, then becomes a part of the strategy statement. Including a name and a due date aids in monitoring the strategy's implementation and in assuring that a key executive "owns" each strategy.

Post-Planning Implementation Steps

Following development of your strategies, you have additional opportunities to encourage successful implementation. You can:

1. Develop a detailed action plan for each of your strategies.
2. Make sure that the strategies and the organizational structure are compatible.
3. Consider the necessary human resource issues related to strategy implementation.
4. Assure that the necessary resources are allocated to each strategy through the annual budgeting process.
5. Stay in control of your strategies through an ongoing monitoring process.
6. Maintain the necessary linkages, that is, make sure that all elements of the organization are working together toward the successful implementation of your strategy.

These six supporting factors of strategy implementation are the subject of the next chapter.

41

Strategy Implementation—Six Supporting Factors

Organizations effective at *strategy implementation* successfully manage six strategy-supporting factors: action planning, organization structure, human resources, the annual business plan, monitoring and control, and linkage (see Figure 41-1).

Action Planning

First, organizations successful at strategy implementation develop detailed action plans, chronological lists of action steps or tactics that add the necessary detail to strategies, and assign responsibility to a specific individual for accomplishing each of those steps. Also, they set a due date and estimate the resources required to accomplish each of the action steps. Thus, they translate their broad strategy statement into a number of *specific* work assignments. In the next chapter, we'll take a close look at the action plan.

Figure 41-1. Strategy implementation—six supporting factors.

1. Action Planning
2. Organization
3. Human Resources
4. Annual Business Plan
5. Monitoring and Control

Organization Structure

Next, successful implementers give thought to their organizational structure and ask if their intended strategy is appropriate for that structure. And they ask a deeper question as well: "Is the organizational structure appropriate to the intended strategy?"

Here's an example. A mid-western company was experiencing problems implementing a strategy calling for the development of two new products. The reason the company had been unable to develop those products was simple: It had never organized to do so. Lacking the necessary commitment for new product development, management didn't establish an R&D group. Rather, it assigned its manufacturing engineering group the job of new product development and hired two junior engineers for the task. Since the primary function of the manufacturing engineering group was to keep the factory humming, those engineers kept getting pulled off their "new product" projects into the role of the manufacturing support. Result: no new products.

Human Resources

Organizations successful at implementation consider the human resource factor in making strategies happen. Further, they realize that the human resource issue is really a two-part story. First, consideration of human resources requires that management think about the organization's communication needs and that it articulate the strategies so that those charged with developing the corresponding action steps fully understand the strategy their tactics are to implement.

Second, managers successful at implementation are aware of the effects each new strategy will have on their human resource needs. They ask themselves the questions, "How much change does this strategy call for?" and "How quickly must we provide for that change?" Another question they consider is, "What are the human resource implications of our answers to those two questions?"

In Chapter 43, we'll take a careful look at these questions. Your answers will help you decide whether to allow time for your employees to grow through experience, to introduce training, or to hire new employees.

The Annual Business Plan

Organizations successful at implementation are aware of their need to fund their intended strategies, and they begin to think about that necessary financial commitment early in the planning process. First, they "ballpark" the financial requirements when they first develop their strategy; later, when developing their action plans, they "firm up" that commitment. As one manager explains, they "dollarize" their strategy. That way, they link their strategic plan to their annual business plan (and their budget). And they eliminate the "surprises" they would otherwise receive at budgeting time.

Monitoring and Control

The monitoring and control function includes a periodic look to see if you're on course; it also includes a list of options to get you back on course if you should veer off. Those options (listed in order of increasing seriousness) include changing the schedule, changing the action steps, changing the strategy, or (as a last resort) changing the objective. More on these options in Chapter 45, where we discuss monitoring your strategic plan.

Linkage—The Foundation for Everything Else

Many organizations put together the above five supports for implementing strategy. They develop action plans, consider organizational structure, take a close look at their human resource needs, fund their strategies through their annual business plan, and develop a plan to monitor and control the accomplishment of their strategies and tactics. Yet they still fail to implement successfully those strategies and tactics. The reason, most often, is they lack *linkage* or the tying together of all the activities of the organization to make sure that all of the organizational resources are rowing in the same direction.

It isn't enough to manage one, two, or a few strategy-supporting factors. To implement your strategies successfully, you've got to manage them all and make sure you link them together.

Strategies require linkage both vertically and horizontally. Vertical linkages establish coordination and support between corporate, divisional, and departmental plans. For example, a divisional strategy calling for development of a new product should be driven by a corporate objective—growth, perhaps—and on a knowledge of available resources—capital resources available from corporate as well as human and technological resources in the R&D department.

Linkages that are horizontal—across departments, across regional offices, across manufacturing plants or divisions—require coordination and cooperation to get the organizational units all playing in harmony. For example, a strategy calling for the introduction of a new product requires the combined efforts of—and thus coordination and cooperation among—the R&D, the marketing, and the manufacturing departments.

In Chapter 44, we'll look further at the subject of linkage.

42
Action Planning

"We think in generalities,
but we live in detail."

—Alfred North Whitehead

Whitehead's right. And his observation certainly applies to strategic planning. When planning, you first develop broad strategies. Then you develop specific steps to accomplish each of those strategies. That's what *action planning* is all about (see Figure 42-1).

Who Develops the Action Plan?

First, you'll need to decide *who* will develop the action plan. We're often asked if the team-planning approach we used earlier to develop the strategic plan can also be used to develop action plans. The answer is a definite "yes." In fact, the same benefits are available to those employing the team-planning approach whether they're developing their strategic plan or their action plans. Those benefits include the broader input contributed by a greater number of individual participants.

A less obvious, but equally important, advantage of

Figure 42-1. The action plan.

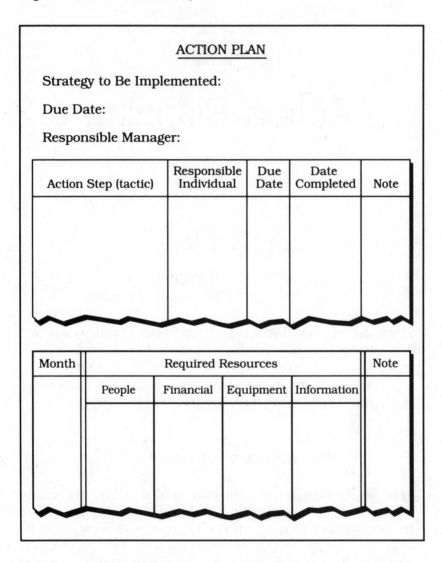

ACTION PLAN

Strategy to Be Implemented:

Due Date:

Responsible Manager:

Action Step (tactic)	Responsible Individual	Due Date	Date Completed	Note

Month	Required Resources				Note
	People	Financial	Equipment	Information	

the team-planning approach is the commitment which comes from participation. Those involved develop a vested interest in seeing the plan through to its successful implementation.

The action-planning team will be led by the manager responsible for the strategy which the action plan is to accomplish. Members of the team will include those whose assistance is required to implement the strategy—that is, to accomplish each of the action steps. Often, the members of the action-planning team will include those from two or more departments within the organization.

What's the Strategy?

If your strategy is not clearly written or if it's too general and thus subject to interpretation, you'll need to rewrite it prior to developing your action steps. And you'll need to discuss it with those responsible for its implementation to make sure they understand it. Then you can begin to develop your action steps.

Who's Responsible?

To monitor the action plan, it's an absolute necessity that someone "sign up" as taking responsibility for it. You must know whom to ask how it's going and whom to offer help to if, for whatever reason, the strategy isn't being accomplished. The manager responsible for the action plan is the same person responsible for the strategy the action plan is intended to implement. And that person signed up for that responsibility way back at the strategy sessions. Remember Marty Marketeer?

What Action Steps?

The action plan includes a list of the action steps (tactics) listed in chronological order. Those steps, taken together, accomplish the intended strategy. Clearly written action steps are essential. You need to know (and agree upon) *exactly* what is to be accomplished.

At one company, the management team had earlier developed an action plan calling for the marketing manager to investigate and report upon a particular market opportunity. When the due date for that action step arrived, the company president asked the marketing manager for that report, fully expecting to receive a *written* report complete with an in-depth analysis.

Instead, the marketing manager replied, "That opportunity isn't all we earlier thought it to be. I suggest we forget it." The president asked, "Have you developed a written report?" "No," was the reply, "but I told you all about it at lunch last Thursday. Don't you remember?"

Don't fall victim to different perceptions of what's due. Make sure each action step is clearly written and agreed to by the manager responsible for its accomplishment.

Who's Responsible For Each Step?
And When Is It Due?

Just as you required a leader to take responsibility for the overall action plan, you also need someone to take responsibility for each step within the action plan. Remember, if you don't reduce the steps to work assignments, they won't happen. And to reduce them to work assignments, you've got to put someone's name on them.

We once worked with a particular client company in a service industry. That company had an employee who, while extremely capable in his field of specialization, had one managerial flaw. He failed to assign specific responsibilities to individuals. Instead, he'd suggest, "We've got to . . ." or "We'd better . . ." or "We need to. . . ." And that's as close to a statement of work as he'd get. This lack of direction created problems for those who worked for him, for they would come out of meetings not knowing who was to do what. No wonder the organization had suffered implementation problems.

You need to determine when each of the action steps is due, who's going to accomplish them, and which steps logically come before others. Then you can list them in chronological order and avoid trying to do them all at the same time. You can allocate resources in a logical order and later use your chronological list for monitoring implementation.

What Resources Are Required?

Naturally, you're going to employ resources to accomplish each of your action steps. Those resources include funding, facilities and equipment, people, and information.

You'll need to quantify the specific resources required to complete each of those action steps. And the earlier you do so, the better job you'll later be able to do in their allocation.

Although most managers focus primarily on the financial resources (an obvious one, admittedly), the resource that turns up scarce more often than any other is the human resource. Most often you just plain run out of time or talent—or time of your most talented people.

That brings up a related issue—"front end loading." The vast majority of plans suffer from promising too much too soon. And it's no surprise. Managers become so enthusiastic about accomplishing their plan that they tend to promise all of it in the near term.

Think about the resources required. Itemize those resources on your action plan, and be realistic about what you can accomplish by when.

The implementation of most complex (and generally the more significant) strategies requires the collective efforts of two or more departments. Here, each department must develop its own list of action steps and also consider the action steps of the other departments on which its own performance is dependent. For example, a strategy calling for development of a new product would involve efforts (action steps) by the R&D, marketing, and production departments, with the activities of each clearly dependent on those of the other two. To implement such strategies, management must encourage interdepartmental communication, understanding, and cooperation. And obviously, the action-planning team must include members from the various departments.

43

People and Change

Implementing strategy implies change. In fact, you wouldn't even develop a strategy if you didn't want to change something—presumably for the better.

But many employees feel threatened by change for a variety of reasons. Those in senior positions, with a well-established power base, may fear a redistribution of their authority. Others may feel threatened by the measurement system which necessarily accompanies strategy implementation. At the very least, all are apprehensive about a disruption of the routine.

Apprehensive or not, individuals respond to strategy implementation in different ways. Some welcome it; others don't. Their degree of acceptance or rejection is dependent on a number of factors: differing perspectives based on their position within the organization, varying levels of risk tolerance, different educational and intellectual preparedness, and differing inclinations to focus on short-term versus long-term objectives.

Reasons Employees Resist Strategy Implementation

Those who resist the impelementation of strategy do so for three fundamental reasons. Some fear their own (or others') inability to successfully implement the strategy.

In dealing with the concern, management must work to increase employee self-confidence by providing the necessary training to improve employee skills and offering encouragement through ongoing communications. Finally, management needs to ensure that allocated resources are sufficient to support successful implementation and that employees understand that those resources are sufficient. Here again, communication is vital.

A second reason that employees resist implementation is their fear that the strategy simply won't work, that is, even if successfully implemented, the strategy won't achieve its intended objectives. To counter employees' concern (whether spoken or unspoken) that the strategy may not work, management must sell employees its (broader) point of view and persuade them that it is right. Hopefully, gentle persuasion will work; as a last resort, stronger persuasion—"Buy into the strategy or we'll find someone who will"—may be necessary.

Still other employees fear that, once implemented, the strategy will work against their own personal goals. To address such concerns, management must deal with employee attitudes and values. Here, management needs to persuade employees that their individual payoffs will be greater than they earlier expected. And if those payoffs aren't greater, management might want to change the reward system in order to better motivate the individuals whose cooperation will be necessary to the successful implementation of strategy.

Though still in the minority, more and more companies are linking financial compensation to strategy implementation, and that seems to make sense. After all, what better way to align the organization's objectives with those of the individuals who must accomplish them?

Be careful, though. Compensation systems require careful consideration. There can be problems—like when a strategy has grown obsolete but those to be compensated for its successful implementation continue to push it. Or when a strategy based on a planning team's faulty assumption can't be implemented—and the one individual assigned responsibility suffers financially.

Financial rewards, while generally an effective motivating factor, frequently aren't the whole story. Not all employees desire only extrinsic rewards (pay, promotion, security). Many individuals, particularly the more highly educated, seek intrinsic rewards (self-satisfaction) primarily. In linking financial compensation to implementation, judgment is crucial.

Communications

No matter which form of resistance to implementation they encounter, managers can make good use of communication, the one common denominator that helps in each case.

It's important to note that communications works both ways—both telling (speaking or writing) and listening. Too many managers forget about the listening part.

It's particularly important for managers to listen. That's how they learn about employees' feelings concerning a particular strategy, about their level of enthusiasm, about their concerns regarding implementation, about their fears. And it's possible that an employee can offer an important insight.

A few years ago, a major beverage company developed a plan to construct a bottling plant on the West Coast. In developing that plan, top management worked directly with the architectural and contracting firms but never thought about including mid- and lower-level employees, the folks responsible for operating the bottling machines, stacking the cases for shipping, or driving the delivery trucks.

When the multimillion-dollar construction project was complete, a few hundred production workers showed up for work. The truck drivers took one look at the loading area and reported that they couldn't back their trucks into the loading dock; the distance between the building and a block wall along the driveway was too small to allow for the wide turns necessary to back in a semi-truck. The truck drivers recognized this problem immediately. But management never thought to ask them about it.

The bottling plant finally did open—after some months and some additional hundreds of thousands of dollars spent on plans, permits, and reconstruction. All were unnecessary expenditures, easily avoided if management had only listened to the folks who had known all along.

It's also important to remember that communication is an ongoing process—not just a single memo or a brief meeting to announce a strategy but an ongoing process beginning well before strategy development and continuing throughout the strategy's successful implementation.

As for the specific form of communication—one-on-one meetings, discussion group sessions, or written documents—it depends on the specific situation. While it's impossible to make universal recommendations regarding how much of each type of communication to use, we can make some general observations.

One-on-one meetings are useful for focusing on specifics: specific individuals' commitment, their perceptions, their fears, the tasks they'll need to perform. Group meetings are helpful for gathering input, for brainstorming ideas, for building consensus. And written documents serve to make official announcements of a final strategic plan, a completed budget, or a project schedule.

Options for Change

At times, to implement a strategy you'll have to add to the skill level of your employees.

There are three options for stimulating such change. First, you can allow your employees to grow through experience. This choice offers the advantages inherent in evolutionary change—it's nonthreatening and supportive of the existing culture. The disadvantage, of course, is that evolutionary change is very slow. Thus it's generally not appropriate for a revolutionary strategy like shifting from low to high technology, from industrial to consumer marketing, or from internal growth to growth through acquisition.

A second method of changing employee skill level is to retrain. It's faster but more costly than the evolutionary method. It's also important to consider what's realistic, that is, who can be retrained to do what and how quickly. Training production workers to program automated assembly equipment is one thing; training them to design such equipment is quite another.

Finally, you can change your employee skill level by hiring one or more new employees. This method has the advantage of bringing on change much faster. But the risks include those of significant cultural change. And you need to be careful to keep your expectations realistic. Too many managers hope to cure all their problems by hiring "the great white knight." The new marketing manager, yet to be hired, will research the market, specify the new product line, train the sales staff, decide on an appropriate level of market diversity, and solve the customer service problem—all within fourteen months. Be careful.

44

Linkage—The Foundation for Everything Else

Suppose you're conducting an orchestra. You'll need to integrate the talents of a number of musicians. Some will play the violin; others the oboe; others the drum. While the contribution of each musician is unique, all work in harmony toward one common objective—the successful performance of the musical piece.

Implementing a strategy is exactly the same. It requires the collective efforts of multiple organizational units, each working on different activities but all working toward a common goal—implementation of the strategy. This process is called *linkage*.

The trick, of course, is to link the activities of the various organizational units to ensure that their collective efforts work in harmony. You'll need to tie together their activities so they provide strategic focus and point in the same direction—toward the successful implementation of the strategy.

Implementation of strategies requires linkage in two dimensions, vertical and horizontal. Vertical linkages are those tying together the organization from top to bottom, from corporate to division to department. For example, if the corporate strategy calls for growth through product development, the division plans had better commit capital to research and development. And the R&D departments within each division will need to remain on the leading edge of appropriate technologies.

Horizontal linkages relate the activities of departments, of regional offices, of manufacturing plants or divisions. The linkages establish coordination and cooperation so that the collective efforts of the various departments can bring about the successful implementation of the strategy. As an example, a strategy calling for computerization of manufacturing would require the collective (and cooperative) efforts of production and human resources.

Another example: In support of a product development strategy, the R&D department will obviously need to be familiar with applicable technologies, and the human resource department will have to recruit those with the applicable technical skills.

One company that was reporting difficulties implementing a growth strategy based on superior service turned out to exhibit a lack of linkage in the organization. The production department was focusing on reducing costs, by itself a commendable goal. But the marketing department wasn't stressing price; rather, it was pushing on both superior service (the firm's stated strategy) and product reliability. And the R&D department wasn't focusing on services or cost or reliability but rather on inventing significant contributions to technology.

Each department's focus was, by itself, complete, but none was linked to the strategy of "increasing market share through superior service." And they certainly weren't linked to each other. Clearly, the organization lacked linkage.

Through proper design of your planning process, you can encourage the establishment of linkages. You'd best develop your plans beginning at the top of the organization and work your way down, from corporate to division to department. In that manner, planning will move from top to bottom, from the more general to the more specific. And each successive level in the organization will have the benefit of direction from above before developing its own plan.

Another excellent way to encourage linkage is to establish action-planning teams which cross departments. That way, people from one department not only appreciate the activities being performed by those in other departments but they better understand the big picture—the strategy in its entirety—and better understand how their own efforts work toward successful strategy implementation.

Finally, you can encourage by communicating—not just an occasional memo describing a strategy but serious, honest-to-goodness, eyeball-to-eyeball discussions on what the strategy is, how in the world you're going to accomplish it, how each person's efforts fit into the big picture.

Some years ago, at a large division of Hewlett-Packard Corporation in Northern California, the division manager was making his monthly presentation to every manager in the division. There he was, up on the stage in a large auditorium, reviewing sales achievements, manufacturing efficiencies, new-product development schedules, and more. All before an audience of three or four hundred managers. And his communication wasn't one-way, either. He fielded questions and took comments from the managers. In all, the presentation took an hour or so.

And that monthly meeting for all managers was only a part of his communications efforts. He met with his immediate staff far more frequently. And in typical Hewlett-Packard fashion, he did his fair share of "managing by wandering around."

It's easy to tell when an organization has a high degree of linkage. Just interview the managers one at a time. Each manager will describe the firm's strategy in some detail. You'll note that the manager has thought carefully about the strategy's implementation and can articulate the specific role of not only his or her own department but of each of the other departments in its successful implementation. And the manager will speak of the specific challenges which each department must face as they relate to implementation. Each of the managers is thus able to take a more "general management overview" of the business.

45

Monitoring the Implementation of the Strategic Plan

An important part of strategy implementation is *monitoring*—taking periodic looks at how you're coming along in implementing your strategic plan.

Monitoring is important because it helps to assure that your efforts conform to the plan, that you're actually performing the action steps you intended.

In addition, monitoring helps you to be sure the results you achieve correspond to your quantified objectives.

Monitoring also allows for corrective action, for making the necessary changes along the way that "fine-tune" not only your strategies but your planning process as well.

Since monitoring is part of a control process, it encourages improved performance. Knowing they'll be measured stimulates employees to do a better job. Thus, through mid-course correction, monitoring helps produce better plans.

Finally, and most importantly, monitoring provides the essential link between the written plan and the day-to-day operation of the business. Monitoring the plan makes your entire planning effort a tangible reality rather than a once-a-year academic exercise.

An "Early Warning" System

A significant benefit of the monitoring process is that it serves as your "early warning system," providing feedback among the functional units and the various levels of the organization on how they are doing and where the problems and opportunities lie.

For example, in developing a new product, the R&D department may run into a technical problem and slip its schedule by six weeks. The marketing department needs to know about it. So does the production department. Through such feedback, you improve the implementation of your strategies and reinforce the spirit of cooperation within our organization.

Getting "Back on Track"

When things do go wrong and some of your action steps are off target, you can take one of four corrective actions. First, you can apply pacing—changing the schedule. Second, you can change the tactics you're using to implement your strategy. Third, you can change your strategy. Finally, as a last resort, you can compromise your objective. Each of these corrective actions is applicable under specific circumstances.

You'd apply pacing to slip your schedule if you felt your fundamental strategy and the tactics you were using to implement it were still sound but simply needed more time. Perhaps you were earlier overly optimistic in deciding on your due date, or perhaps some other activity is temporarily competing for a critical resource. Maybe you decided to wait for some important piece of information—a market survey, a competitive announcement, the opinion of a newly hired manager. All are perfectly valid reasons for pacing.

But be careful. You can't always apply pacing, because the world around you is changing. Competition introduces new products and services. Technology continues to advance. And the needs of your customers change as well. For every strategy there's a "strategic window," a period of time during which the strategy will work. But if you slip your schedule too far, your strategy simply won't work.

Another way to handle an implementation problem is to change your tactics. You'd do that if you believed your fundamental strategy was sound but your tactics for accomplishing it were faulty or the people assigned to accomplish those tactics were the wrong people. Perhaps your marketing department really doesn't have the time to conduct the survey it committed to. Or the production department really doesn't have the expertise to automate the line. In either case, you might continue with your strategy but modify your action steps—by using expertise from outside the organization, for example.

Next, you might consider changing your fundamental strategy. You'd do so if your problem wasn't the schedule or the specific action steps but rather that, for one reason or another, your strategy was simply wrong. Either you earlier developed the wrong strategy or your external environment has changed—customers' needs, competitive offerings, legislative factors, or the economy, perhaps. Or internally, your organization has changed, perhaps through the acquisition of a new asset or a change in availability of a critical resource. These are all valid reasons to change your strategy.

An important distinction between modifying an action step and modifying a strategy is that when you change your action step, you do so because you've been doing the right thing wrong. When you change your strategy, you do so because you've been doing the wrong thing. Big difference.

As a last resort, you may decide to compromise your objective. Here, you'd agree to "accomplish less."

Deciding how much variation should trigger corrective action—and specifically what that corrective action should be—is where managerial judgment counts most and where you get to exercise the art of strategy implementation.

Fine-Tuning the Process

Finally, you should watch for opportunities to "fine-tune" your planning process. This will help with implementation of your strategies in later years. You might, for example, at the third quarterly review of your strategic plan, take a little extra time to discuss the planning *process*, to look back on your strategy development sessions and consider what went well and what didn't. You might also look at changes you could make next time around to improve the plan and its implementation to better fit your company's specific needs.

46

Checking for Focus and Commitment

To help you determine whether your strategies are well-focused and whether your employees are committed to implementing those strategies, we've devised a checklist to help you review your plan.

A. Thinking Strategically About Your Business

1. Have you uncovered your key success factors—your industry-specific answers to the question, "What does it take to win?" Does your entire management team share an understanding of those key success factors? Have you developed a limited number of strategies that focus on maintaining excellence in those key areas of success?

2. Are you really doing something different—differentiating your product, focusing on a specific market segment, or changing the rules of the game? Or are you simply providing a "me too" product or service and hoping for the best?

3. Do your new products and services build on your company's expertise in technology, in operations, and in marketing? Or do they call for an entirely different set

of strengths? Remember, the more different your new products and services are from your current products and services, the greater their risk of failure.

4. How about your relationships with customers? Their loyalty is your greatest asset. What are you doing to earn customer loyalty?

5. Are you using business models to think deeply about your business? They can offer excellent "food for thought." Caution, though—even the 80-20 rule works only 80 percent of the time.

6. Is your business "processlike" or "projectlike"? Or is it a combination of both? Do you know which functions of your business are processlike and which are projectlike? Do you manage the two distinct types of operations differently? How about standards versus specials—which do you provide? Are you managing your business accordingly?

7. Do you hire and retain the "right" people? Do you support those people with adequate resources and a healthy level of "neglect" so they can grow and develop? And do you delegate properly by telling employees what you'd like them to accomplish and allowing them to discover how to accomplish it?

8. Do you consider each individual employee's specific strengths and weaknesses? Do you know which of your key managers is a "hunter," a "farmer," a "shepherd"? Do you assign them responsibilities which build on their specific strengths?

9. If you're operating a family business, are you careful to keep family objectives separate from business objectives? Do you require family-member employees to earn their positions in the organization just as non-family-member employees have to do?

10. If your company's stock is publicly traded, are you paying more attention to the price of that stock than you are to operating the business—to delivering quality in your products and services and offering value to your

customers? If so, wouldn't you be better off concentrating on quality and value and trust that the price of the stock will take care of itself?

11. Sure, you've got some problems in your business. So has everyone else. The trick is to discover those problems and solve them once. Are you good at identifying those fundamental problems by asking the right questions and by solving your problems just once?

B. Getting Ready for Planning

1. Have you selected the "right" managers as members of your planning team? Remember the two criteria: Each must be able to contribute to the development of a complete, high-quality strategic plan, and each must be positioned to drive the successful implementation of the strategies within the plan.

2. Have you educated the members of your planning team to the strategic planning process? Have you built their enthusiasm and balanced that enthusiasm with realistic expectations?

3. Prior to your strategy sessions, do you make use of one or more pre-planning forms? They'll make your sessions much more efficient, they'll get your planning team members thinking strategically, and they'll provide a safe way to bring up controversial issues.

4. Prior to planning, are you gathering the "right" information and are you sharing that information with everyone on your planning team, thus developing a common understanding in preparation for your strategy sessions?

5. Have you thought about the time span of your strategic plan? Is the correct time span three years, five years, ten years? What factors led you to that conclusion?

C. While Developing Your Strategy

1. Do you hold your planning meetings at an off-site location? Is your planning team free from interruptions?

2. When discussing your internal strengths and weaknesses, are you comparing your company against its competition? You should. A good way to do so is to make use of the bell-shaped curve.

3. When listing your organization's internal weaknesses, are you really getting at the fundamental weaknesses, or does your weakness list contain a number of "symptoms" as well?

4. In itemizing your external opportunities, are you careful to keep strategies from sneaking onto the list? Remember, opportunities are external; they're independent of the existence of your organization. Strategies require action—they're "we're doing" statements. Save your strategies for a later step in the process.

5. Have you developed a short, succinct mission statement? Does it describe your business from two directions—from the inside out and from the outside in? Is it descriptive of the product or service you offer and the functions you perform in offering those products or services? Does it describe the market you serve and position your firm in the marketplace by describing why customers choose to buy your products or services?

6. How about your objectives? Are they "in balance," not all related to finance and marketing, of interest to the folks "at the top only," but addressing products, services, and people? Keep in mind that most of the folks whose help you'll need in implementing your strategy care more about products, services, and people than they do about finance and marketing.

7. Have you quantified each of your objectives? If an objective isn't quantified, you won't be able to measure it. And if you don't measure it, it won't happen.

D. Implementing Your Strategy

1. Are you linking your strategic plan to management by objectives? Along with each strategy, do you list a responsible manager and a due date? Even the best

strategy won't happen by itself. You've got to reduce it to a work assignment.

2. Did the manager responsible for each strategy develop an action plan detailing that strategy's implementation? Did that manager create the action plan with the help of those who will assist in its implementation?

3. Did you assure that the strategies you developed were compatible with your organizational structure and with your company culture? For a strategy to succeed, its environment must be "friendly."

4. Have you considered the human resource issues related to strategy implementation? Do you have the work force and the expertise to implement your strategy? Do your employees have fears which you'll need to address before those fears become blockages to implementation? And have you included ongoing communications as part of your implementation plan?

5. To implement your strategy, will you need to build the skill level of your employees? Have you considered your various options: growth through experience, retraining, and hiring new employees? Which should you choose? Why?

6. Have you ensured, through your budgeting process, that the resources are really committed to supporting each of your strategies?

7. Have you committed to an ongoing monitoring process to make sure you stay on track in implementing your strategies?

8. Do you maintain the necessary linkages within your organization so all of your organization's energies are "pushing" in the same direction—toward the successful implementation of your strategy?

Bibliography

Abell, D. F., and J. S. Hammond, *Strategic Market Planning: Problems and Analytical Approaches.* Englewood Cliffs, N.J.: Prentice-Hall, 1979.

Buzzell, R. D., and B. T. Gale, *The PIMS Principles: Linking Strategy to Performance.* New York: Free Press, 1987.

Deal, T. E., and A. A. Kennedy, *Corporate Cultures.* Reading, Mass.: Addison-Wesley, 1982.

Donaldson, Gordon, and Jay W. Lorsch, *Decision Making at the Top: The Shaping of Strategic Direction.* New York: Basic Books, 1983.

Drucker, Peter F., *Managing in Turbulent Times.* New York: Harper & Row, 1980.

Freeman, R. E., *Strategic Management: A Stakeholder Approach.* Aulander, N.C.: Pittman Publishing, 1984.

Galbraith, Jay R., and Daniel Nathanson, *Strategy Implementation: The Role of Structure and Process.* St. Paul: West Publishing Co., 1978.

Guth, W. D., *Handbook of Business Strategy.* New York: Warren Gorham & Lamont, 1985.

Hawken, P., *The Next Economy.* Fort Worth, Tex.: Holt, Rinehart & Winston, 1983.

Henderson, Bruce D., *Henderson on Corporate Strategy.* Cambridge, Mass.: Abt Books, 1979.

Kanter, R. M., *The Change Masters: Innovations for Productivity in the American Corporation.* New York: Simon & Schuster, 1983.

Kastens, M. T., *Long-Range Planning for Your Business.* New York: AMACOM, 1976.

———, *Maintaining Momentum in Long-Range Planning.* New York: AMACOM, 1984.

Levitt, T., *The Marketing Imagination.* New York: Free Press, 1983.

Linneman, R. E., *Shirt-Sleeve Approach to Long-Range Planning, for the Smaller, Growing Corporation.* Englewood Cliffs, N.J.: Prentice-Hall, 1980.

Lorange, Peter, ed., *Implementation of Strategic Planning.* Englewood Cliffs, N.J.: Prentice-Hall, 1982.

Naisbett, J., *Megatrends: New Directions Transforming Our Lives.* New York: Warner Books, 1982.

Naylor, T. H., *Strategic Planning Management.* Oxford, Ohio: Planning Executives Institute, 1980.

Ohmae, K., *The Mind of the Strategist.* New York: McGraw-Hill, 1982.

Peters, R. T., and R. H. Waterman, Jr., *In Search of Excellence.* New York: Harper & Row, 1980.

Porter, M. E., *Competitive Advantage: Creating and Sustaining Superior Performance.* New York: Free Press, 1985.

_____ , *Competitive Strategy: Techniques for Analyzing Industries and Competitors.* New York: Free Press, 1980.

Ries, A., and J. Trout, *Positioning—The Battle for Your Mind.* New York: Warner Books, 1981.

_____ , *Marketing Warfare.* New York: McGraw-Hill, 1986.

Sawyer, G. C., *Corporate Planning as a Creative Process.* Oxford, Ohio: Planning Executives Institute, 1983.

Steiner, George A., *Strategic Planning: What Every Manager Must Know.* New York: Free Press, 1979.

Stonich, P. J., *Implementing Strategy.* Cambridge, Mass.: Ballinger, 1982.

Index

accounting cycle, 140
accounting techniques,
    conventional, 187
action planning, 200, 205
  to encourage linkage, 218
  resources for, 209–210
  responsibility for, 205–209
  steps of, 207–209
  strategy for, 207
activities-oriented objective,
    135
advertising, 15–16
alternatives, evaluation of,
    85
annual business plan, 203
assumptions, planning,
    109–110
  developing, 109–110
  in written plan, 171
AT&T, small facilities of, 55
automation, diminishing
    returns from, 50–51
bell-shaped curve, 120–122
Boston Consulting Group,
    175–186
bottom-up planning, 75–76
break, importance of,
    147–148
business
  nature of, 140
  shortsightedness of,
    123–124
  thinking strategically
    about, 224–226

business plan, annual, 203

capital equipment, changes
    in demand for, 24–25
cash cows, 180–181
Cessna, focus of, 8
change
  communications about,
    213–214
  options for, 214–215
  reasons for resisting,
    211–213
  in skill level, 215
commitment
  building of, 6
  checking for, 228
  importance of, 5–6, 79–81
  lack of, 4
  with team planning,
    79–80
communication
  to encourage linkage, 218
  of information for
    planning, 98–99
Company Emphasis form,
    164–166
Comparative Advantage, Law
    of, 49–52
competition
  normal distribution in,
    120–122
  situation analysis of,
    118–119
computerization, 56